Street by St

HAMPSHIRE

PLUS BOURNEMOUTH, CAMBERLEY, CHRISTCHURCH, FARNHAM, FERNDOWN, HASLEMERE, NEWBURY, NORTH TIDWORTH, POOLE, SOUTHBOURNE, VERWOOD, WIMBORNE MINSTER

Enlarged Areas Aldershot, Andover, Basingstoke, Fareham, Gosport, Havant, Portsmouth, Southampton, Winchester

Ist edition May 2001

© Automobile Association Developments Limited 2001

This product includes map data licensed from Ordnance Survey® with the permission of the Controller of Her Majesty's Stationery Office. © Crown copyright 2000. All rights reserved. Licence No: 399221.

Published by AA Publishing (a trading name of Automobile Association Developments Limited, whose registered office is Norfolk House, Priestley Road, Basingstoke, Hampshire, RG24 9NY. Registered number 1878835).

Mapping produced by the Cartographic Department of The Automobile Association.

ISBN 0 7495 2617 3

A CIP Catalogue record for this book is available from the British Library.

Printed by in Italy by Printer Trento srl

The contents of this atlas are believed to be correct at the time of the latest revision. However, the publishers cannot be held responsible for loss occasioned to any person acting or refraining from action as a result of any material in this atlas, nor for any errors, omissions or changes in such material. The publishers would welcome information to correct any errors or omissions and to keep this atlas up to date. Please write to Publishing, The Automobile Association, Fanum House, Basing View, Basingstoke, Hampshire, RG21 4EA.

Ref: MD011

ii

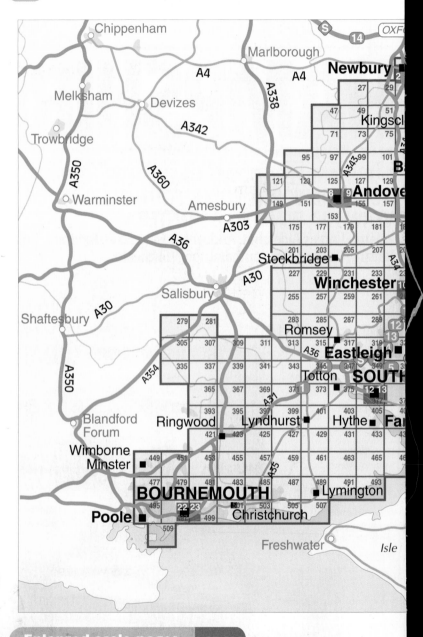

Chippenham

Marlborough

Newbury

A4

A4

A338

Melksham

Devizes

A342

Trowbridge

A350

A360

Warminster

Amesbury

A303

27 29

47 49 51

Kingscl

71 73 75

95 97 A343 99 101 B

121 123 125 127 129

8 9 Andove

149 151 155 157

153

Shaftesbury

A30

A36

A303

A30

Salisbury

175 177 179 181 18

201 203 205 207

Stockbridge

227 229 231 233 A34

255 257 259 261

Winchester

279 281

283 285 287 289 12 13

305 307 309 311 313 315 317 319 3

335 337 339 341 343 A36 Eastleigh

365 367 369 371 373 345 347 349

Totton SOUTH

A31 12 13

393 395 397 399 401 403 405 40

Ringwood Lyndhurst Hythe Fa

421 423 425 427 429 431 433 43

449 451 453 455 457 459 461 463 465 46

477 479 481 483 485 487 489 491 493

BOURNEMOUTH Lymington

495 22 23 501 503 505 507

Poole 499

509 Christchurch

Freshwater Isle

A350

A354

A355

A31

Blandford
Forum

Wimborne
Minster

Enlarged scale pages 1:17,500 3.6 inches to 1 mile

0 1/2 miles 1

0 1/2 1 kilometres 1 1/2

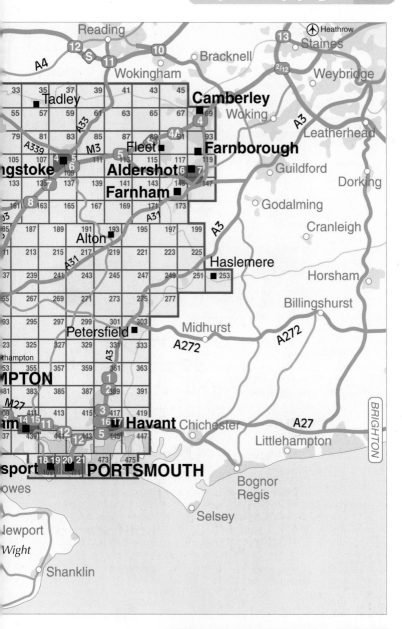

2.5 inches to I mile   **Scale of main map pages   1:25,000**

| 0 | 1/2 | miles | I | | 1 1/2 |

| 0 | 1/2 | I | kilometres | 1 1/2 | 2 |

iv

Junction 9	Motorway & junction
Services	Motorway service area
	Primary road single/dual carriageway
Services	Primary road service area
	A road single/dual carriageway
	B road single/dual carriageway
	Other road single/dual carriageway
	Restricted road
	Private road
← ←	One way street
	Pedestrian street
	Track/footpath
	Road under construction
]= = = ={	Road tunnel
P	Parking

P+	Park & Ride
	Bus/coach station
	Railway & main railway station
	Railway & minor railway station
⊖	Underground station
⊖	Light railway & station
+++++++	Preserved private railway
LC	Level crossing
•—•—•	Tramway
- - - - - -	Ferry route
....	Airport runway
— · — · —	Boundaries-borough/district
◥◣◥◣◥	Mounds
93	Page continuation 1:25,000
7	Page continuation to enlarged scale 1:17,500

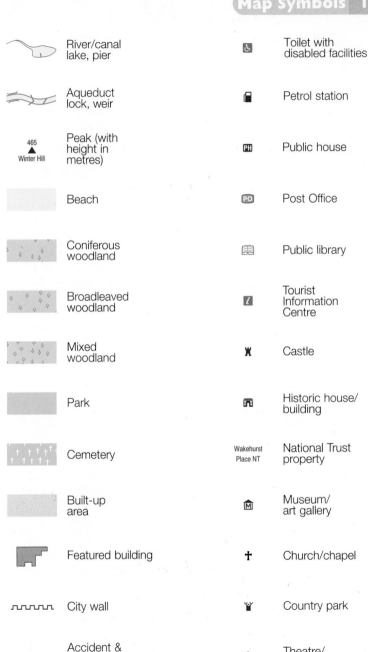

River/canal lake, pier

Aqueduct lock, weir

465
▲
Winter Hill
Peak (with height in metres)

Beach

Coniferous woodland

Broadleaved woodland

Mixed woodland

Park

Cemetery

Built-up area

Featured building

City wall

A&E
Accident & Emergency hospital

Toilet

Toilet with disabled facilities

Petrol station

PH   Public house

PO   Post Office

Public library

i   Tourist Information Centre

Castle

Historic house/ building

Wakehurst
Place NT
National Trust property

M   Museum/ art gallery

†   Church/chapel

Country park

Theatre/ performing arts

Cinema

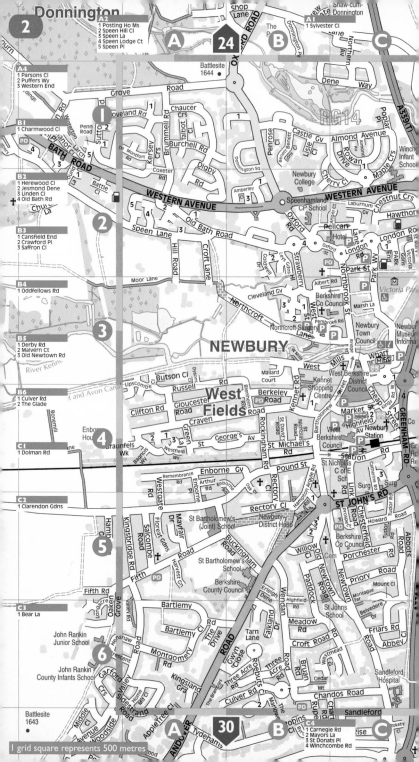

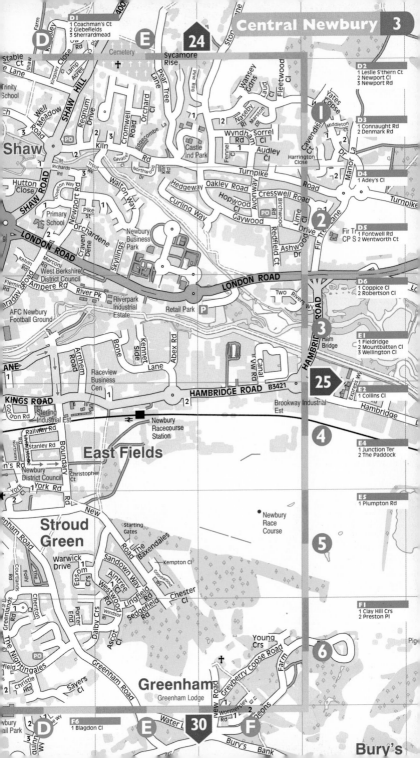

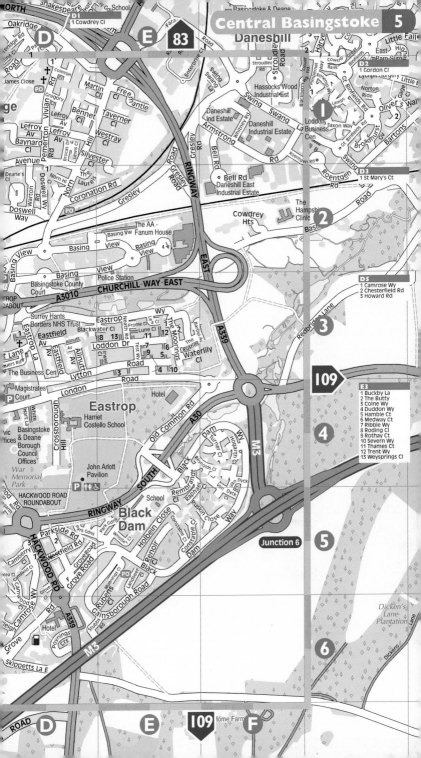

D1
1 Cowdrey Cl

83

Little Fall

D
E

East
Barn Surfe

D2
1 Gordon Cl
Lyophil Surgery
Norton
Ride

Oakridge
Road

James Close

PO

Coleman

Martin
Cl

Freemantle

Gregory

Vivian
Cl

Bennet
Cl

Taverner
Cl

Lefroy
Av

Hassocks Wood
Industrial Est

Loddon
Business
Cen

Saxon Way

Swing

Westray
Cl

Brocas

Lefroy
Av

Baynardes
Cl

Lefroy
Av

Silvester
Cl

The
Laurels

Lewis

Pemberton

Swing

Swing

Bartons

Broadhurst
Gv

Oliver Gage

Norn Hl

Warton

Boswell Hill

Norn

Coronation Rd

PO

Doswell
Way

Daneshill
Ind Estate

Armstrong

Daneshill
Industrial Estate

Whitney Rd

Roentgen Rd

Rd

Oliver Wal
Little t

Avenue

Basing
View

Basing
View

Basing Vw -
Fanum House

The AA -
Fanum House

Basing
View

Basing
View

Basing
View

Gresley Road

Gresley

RINGWAY

EAST

Bell Rd

Bell Rd East
Industrial Estate

Cresley Rd

Cowdrey
Hts

Redbridge Lane

The
Hampshire
Clinic

Basing

D3
1 St Mary's Ct

Road

Roentgen

Rd

I

1

2

D5
1 Camrose Wy
2 Chesterfield Rd
3 Howard Rd

Basingstoke County
Court

A3010

Police Station

CHURCHILL WAY EAST

3

Surrey Hants
Borders NHS Trust

Eastfield
Av

Eastrop

Blackwater Cl

Eastfield

Allnutt
Av

Loddon Dr

Eastfield

Allnutt
Av

Frome Cl

Lune Cl

Irwell
Rd

Test
Rd

The
Moorings

Barrier Av

The
Crushes

Waterlily
Cl

A339

109

E3
1 Buckby La
2 The Butty
3 Colne Wy
4 Duddon Wy
5 Hamble Cl
6 Medway Ct
7 Ribble Wy
8 Roding Cl
9 Rothay Ct
10 Severn Wy
11 Thames Ct
12 Trent Wy
13 Weysprings Cl

8

13

11

12

9

5

6

3

4

10

Magistrates
Court

P

London

Road

Hotel

4

Crossborough Hill

White

Hurt La

Eastrop

Harriet
Costello School

Old Common Rd

A30

War
Memorial
Park

Basingstoke
& Deane
Borough
Council
Offices

John Arlott
Pavilion

P

Dam

Turner Ct

Hoarn

Reynolds Cl

Van Dyck

M3

5

HACKWOOD ROAD
ROUNDABOUT

RINGWAY

SOUTH

School

Rembrandt

Black

Ruskin Close

Constable

Dam

**Black
Dam**

Junction 6

HACKWOOD RD

Parkside Rd

Westfield Rd

Grove Rd

Grove Road

Holbein Close

Stencir

Black

Whistler

Pak Gdns

Dam

PO

Landseer
Ct

Camberly
Cl

Camwood Wy

Grove
Rd

A359

Rubens
Ct

Crainsborough Road

Camrose

Grove

Hotel

Poifnings
Cts

M3

Skippetts La E

6

Dicken's
Lane
Plantation

Dickens
Lane

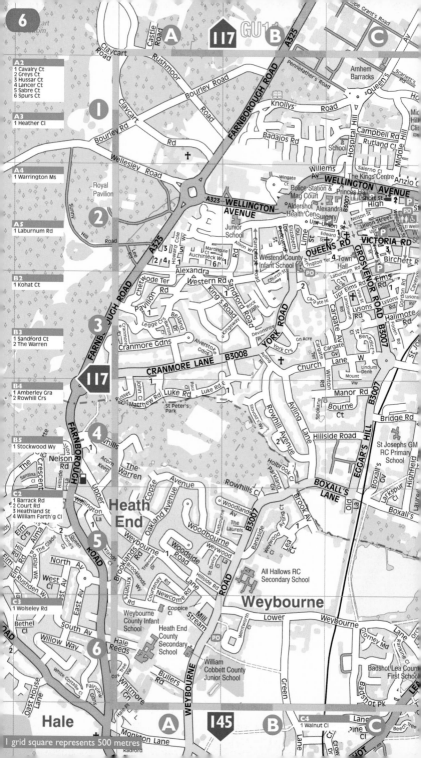

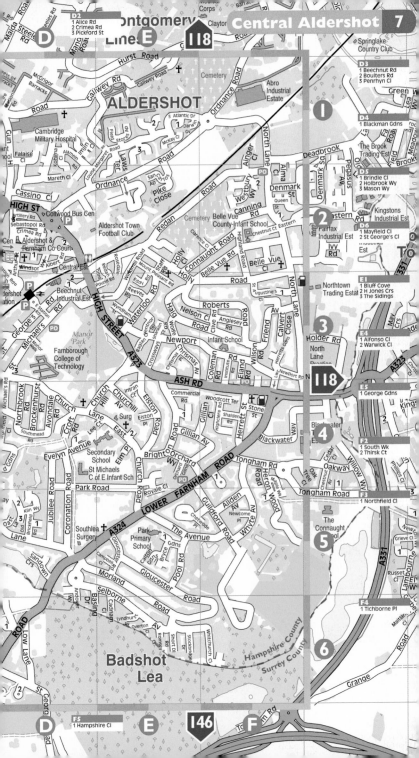

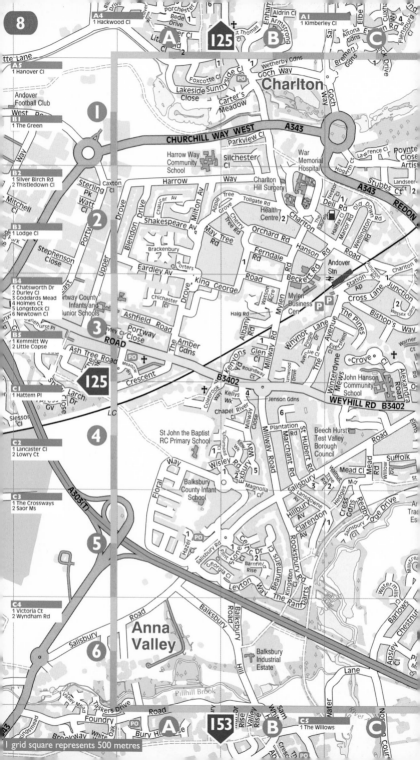

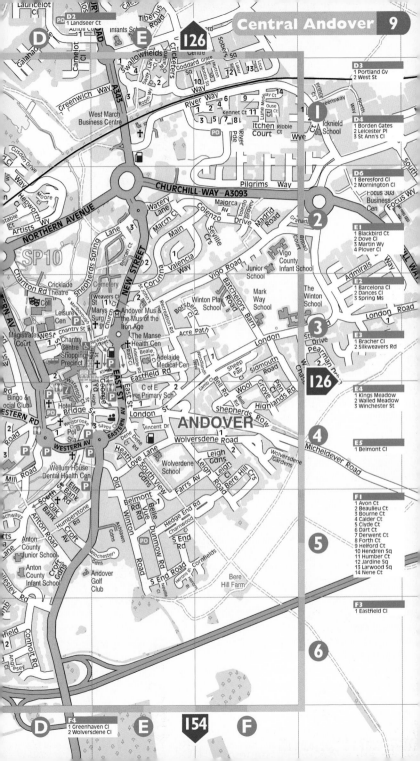

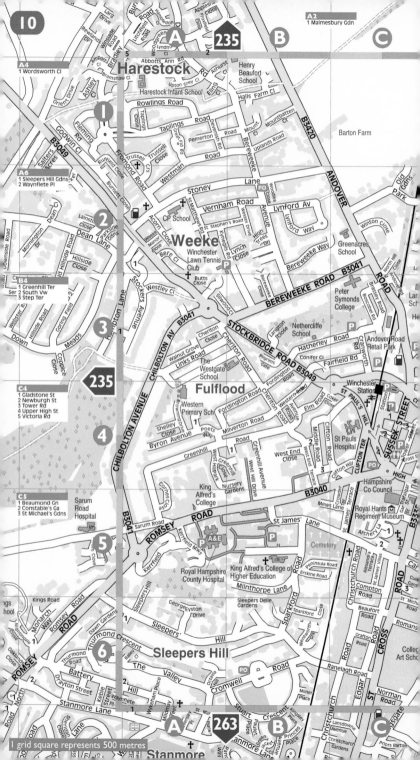

I grid square represents 500 metres

377

D1
1 Augustine Rd
2 Nthumberld Rd

The Alpha
Business Park

Marina

D2
1 Clifford St
2 Guildford St
3 Nichols Rd
4 St Alban's Rd
5 Wolverton Wy

Mount Pleasant Rd
anbury Av
Street
Southampton
Central
Mosque
Meridian TV
Studios

Northam Bridge
Summers St
Prince's Street
Northam
Business
Cen
Millbank
St

Alfred Lwr Alfred
Bullar St
am Rd

Union Rd
Hindu
Temple
Parsonage
Rd
Prince's St
Graham St
Coburg St

Lwr York
St
Bond

PO
Kent
St
York
St

Durnford
Radcliffe
Rd

D3
1 Maryfield

enue
Road

Derby Rd
LC
Northumberland
Hartington Road

Kent
Rd
Peel
St
Primary
School
Belvidere
Victoria Rd
Belvidere Rd

Lwr
William
St

Northam

Willments
Industrial
Est

Braeside Rd
Gainsford
Bryanston Rd

2

D4
1 Paget St
2 Richmond St
3 Royal Cres Rd
4 St Lawrence Rd
5 Saltmarsh Rd

Peartree Avenue

Gasholders
Golden Grove

Southampton FC
(under constr.)

River Itchen

Millhouse
Business
Centre

Peartree
Green

Peartree Rd

D5
1 Atlantic Cl
2 Mermaid Wy

Sholing

rompton
allery

Central
Trading
Est

PO
Golden Grove

messt
Surg
eman St

College

Chapel Rd
Coll

Elm
Street

Hazel Road

Sea Rd

3

Seward Rd
Mullion
Mortimer Rd
Peverill Rd
Woodhouse
North
Ludlow Rd
Manor Rd

Middle
School

E1
1 Campbell St
2 Charliejoy Gdns
3 Princes Ct

Deanery
Campus

Anglesea Ter
Paget St
Andersons

B3038

ALBERT RD N

MELBOURNE STREET
MARINE PDE
BRITANNIA ROAD

Southampton
Technical
College

The Itchen Bridge

Defender Rd

Bridge Rd
Tankerville Rd
Woolston Stn

378

Radstock
Infant
School
Itchen

E4
1 Asturias Wy

Captains
College
Hall of Aviation

CENTRAL BR

Royal
Cr

Albert Rd
Canute Rd
Alcantara Cres

Floating Br
Andes
Close

Longbridge
Ind Park

Spitfire
Court
Surgery

A3025

Garton
Road

Vineyard Cl

4

Patricks RC
Primary
School

Norton
Fort

E5
1 Ocean Wy

CANUTE ROAD
Channel Wy

Calshot Spit
Lightship

Channel
Keswick Rd

Portsmouth Rd
Oakbank Rd
Woolley
Inkerman Rd
John's Rd

PO

West Rd
Enfield Rd

The Canute Surg
The Old Fire

E5
1 Ocean Wy

Ocean
Business
Cen

PO

Regional Film Theatre
SS Shieldhall

Maritime
Tasman Cl
Pacific Cl
Pacific

Ocean Village

Florence Rd

Victoria Road
Woolley
Obelisk
Longmore Rd

First School

Hazeleigh Av
Lyndock
Canada Rd
Anne's Gdns

Woolston

St Anne's Gdns
Bedford Av
Caro
College Road
College Road

5

F2
1 Ashburnham Cl

Oceanographic
Centre

Java Rd

Glen Road
Weston Grove Road
Thornycroft
Holland Rd
Garnock Rd
Lake Rd

Church
Road

Swift

Swift
Gardens

Archery

Swift

Weston

Weston

6

F2
1 Peartree Cl

Unwin
Rd
Itchen
Way

Jurds Lake Way
Arrow Cl
Fulton Rd
Rothschild

Ticonderoga
Bevan Cl

Riversdale
Close

F3
1 Longmore Crs

Duncan Cl

F4
1 Condor Cl
2 Cooper's La
3 Jackmans Cl
4 Shamrock Rd

Weston La

377

River Itchen

F6
1 Dundonald Cl
2 Swift Hollow
3 Victoria Rd
4 Waldegrave Cl

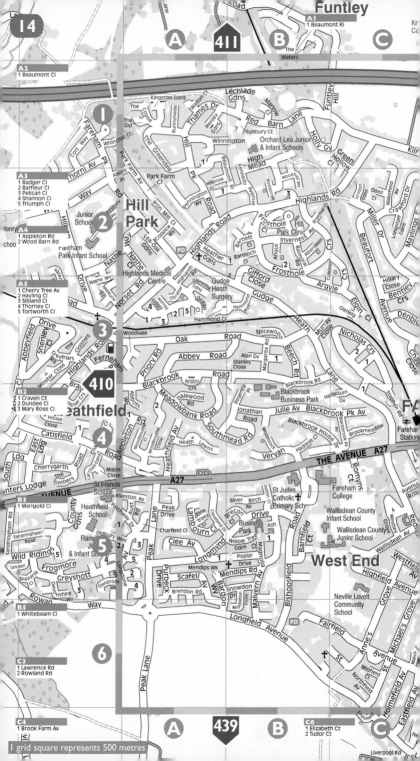

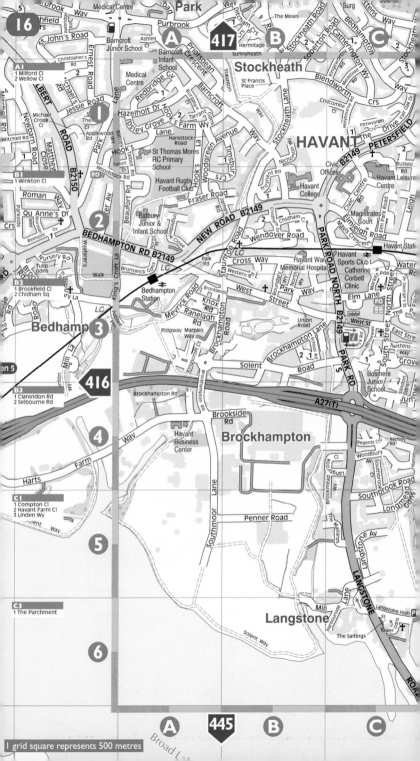

441

D E I

Buckler's Road

City of Portsmouth Hampshire County

2

Shipbuilding Rd
Boiler Rd
Shipbuilding Rd
Victoria
Murray's La
Queen's Rd
King's Rd
Sampson Rd
Scott Rd
Jago Rd

Mary Rose Ship Hall
HMS Victory

Burrow Island

ay

Parham Road
Ferrol Road

Salt Meat
Staff
Orchard La
Gn

Brewhouse Sq

Osborne Rd

Jamaica Rd
Flag Staff
Mewill

Yacht Marina

Royal Naval Museum **D3**
Dockyard Appre
1 Battenburg Rd
2 Carlton Rd
3 Carlton Wy
4 Fey Rd
5 Pearce Ct
Ma

3

Portsmouth Harbour

HMS Warrior
Portsmouth Harbour Station

20

Albert
St
Seaford St
Victoria
George
5
Leonard Rd
Spring Gdn La
A32
Clarence Rd
MUMBY
Harbour Rd
ROAD A32
Minnitt Rd

D4
1 Henery St
2 Joseph St
3 Leventhorpe Ct
4 Molesworth Rd
5 Pr of Wales Rd
6 Stoke Gdns
7 Woodley Rd

Grove AV
Queen's
Avenue
Peel
2 3
1
Newtown
Strathmore Rd
Holly St

Gosport Museum
Walpole Rd
Town Hall
PO
Creek Rd
Oldways Rd
St Cross St
Cross St
N St

SOUTH STREET
Bus Station

4
Portsm
Harbour

Isle o
Car P
Ter

Stoke Road
Stoke Rd
Jamaica Rd
Richard Martin Gallery & Bookshop
2 1
Church Path
The Esplanade
Trinity Cl
Trinity C
City of Portsmouth Hampshire County

PH
Bath St
Bathing La
East

SOUTH ST
The Anchorage
Dock Rd
Woodstock
Shaftsbury
Endeavour Cl
Shamrock Cl
Nyria Wy
Willis Rd

BR
1

D5
1 Thornbrake Rd

Cranbourne Rd
Kensington
Road
1

STREET

Old
Hornet Close
Hilton Rd
Dolman Rd
Dolman Rd
Mariners Wy

5

Dolphin Crescent
field

Haslar Road
Solent Way
PO

Royal Navy Submarine Museum Offices

HMS Dolphin

E4
1 Thorngate Wy

6

Clayhall

Haslar Road

Royal Hospital Haslar

Cemetery

Mabey Cl
Clayhall Rd
Lime Rd
D
Francis Rd
2
The Redan
Waterloo Rd
Dolphin Way
E
470
ISLE OF WIGHT
F
ISLE OF WIGHT

441

A B C

Hampshire County

Burrow

Shipbuilding Rd

Boiler Rd

Navy Rd

HM Naval Base

Aldrich Rd

Victoria

Murray's La

Queen's Rd

The Pde

Marlborough Rd

Gloucester Rd

Anchor Gate

Circular Rd

Mary Rose Ship Hall

HMS Victory

King's Rd

Sampson Rd

Scott Rd

Jago Rd

Stony La

Anchor La

Cumberland St

HMS Nelson

Portsmouth Harbour

Royal Naval Museum

Dockyard Apprentice Exhibition

Mary Rose Exhibition

Sunny Wk

College Rd

Admiralty Rd

Bonfire

Cross St

Kg William St

North St

Pr George St

Portsea

Doctors Surg

Treadgold Mus

St Ce

Port Nor Swi

Portsmouth Harbour

HMS Warrior

Portsmouth Harbour Station

Queen St

St Georges Beneficial C of E Prim Sch

Union St

Curzon Howe Rd

Bishop

University

Kent St

Portland St

St George Rd

Richmond

Butcher St

Victoria Park Swimming Cen

University

United Services Cricket Grnd

Kg Univers

Theatre R

Harbour Rd

B2154

St Georges Park Road

Dean

St Georges Park Business Cen

United Services Business Cen

United Services Rugby Club

Burnaby Road

University of Portsmouth

P

Beehive Wk Solent Way

Isle of Wight Car Ferry Terminal

Armory La

Gunwharf Rd

ST GEORGE'S RD

HMS Temeraire

CAMBRIDGE RD

MUSEUM RD

ST MICHAEL

HAMPSHIRE TERRACE

Grammar Sch

Kin Clini

A 8

The Pasco Practi

Fish Market

Bath Sq

Bathing La East St

Broad St

West St

White Hart Rd

Oyster St

Warblington St

Highbury St

St Thomas's St

Portsmouth City Council

City Mus & Art Gallery

Museum Rd

St Thomas's St

Nat Hea

OLD PORTSMO

Captains Rw

BROAD STREET

Tower St

A3

Penny St

HIGH ST

Goldfield Gallery

Pembroke Rd

Primary Sch

Hth

Highbury Dr

Melville Dr

JUBILEE TERRACE

SOUTHSEA TER BELLEVUE TERR

13.5

Hambre

University

Portsmouth Cathedral Church of St Thomas of Canterbury

St Nicholas St

Chatham Dr

Long Curtain Rd

Solent Way

P

PIER ROAD

A288

Duisburg Way

WEST

Clarence Pier and Amusement Centre

Hovercraft Terminal

Clarence Esp

Southsea Common

Clarence Esplanade

Royal Nav Memoria

Royal Navy Submarine Museum Offices

oyal ospita slar

PO

1 grid square represents 500 metres

19

19

I

2

3

4

5

6

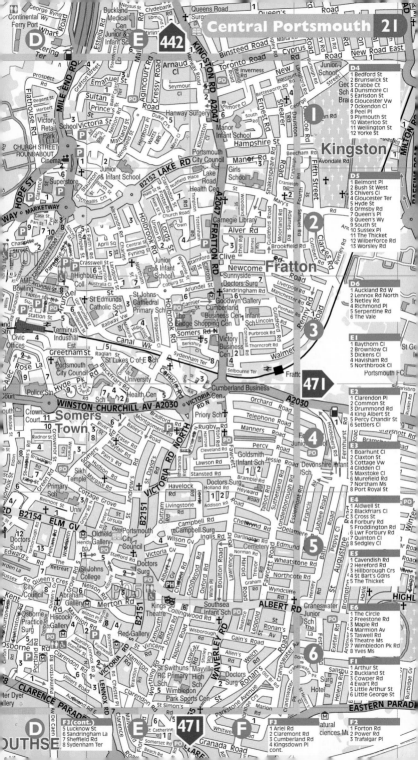

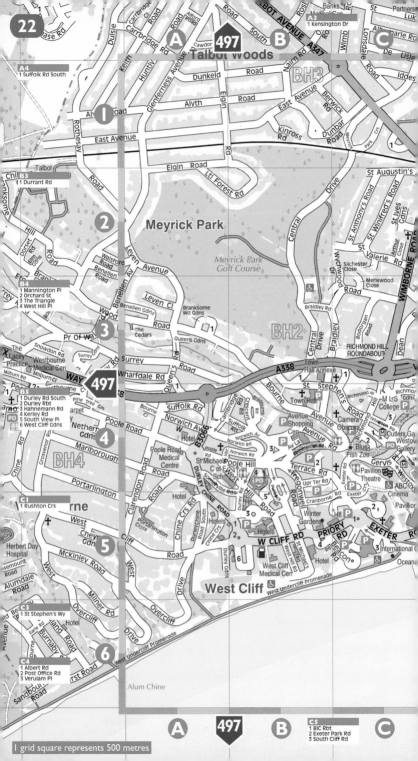

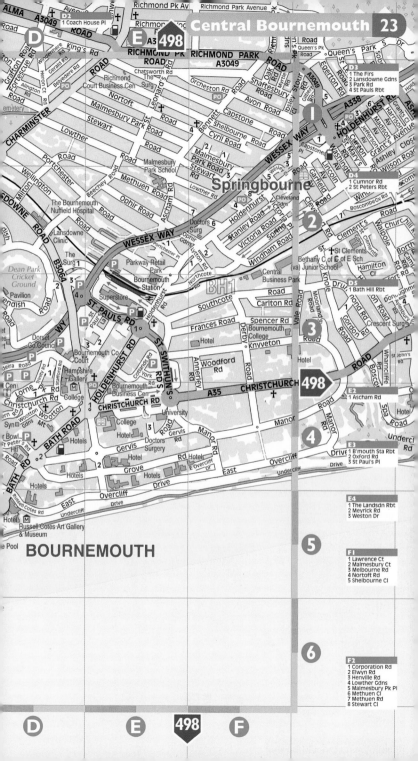

A4
1 Posting Ho Ms
2 Speen Hill Cl
3 Speen La
4 Speen Lodge Ct
5 Speen Pl

A3
1 Sylvester Cl

F3
1 Clay Hill Crs
2 Preston Pl

F8
1 Blagdon Cl

G3
1 Fairfax Pl
2 Pindar Pl

G4
1 Cresswell Rd
2 Ludlow Cl

G6
1 Overbridge Sq

H4
1 Southdown Rd

H5
1 Foxhunter Wy

J5
1 Clerewater Pl
2 Ennerdale Wy
3 Saxon Ct

K4
1 Westland

E6
1 Junction Ter
2 The Paddock

E7
1 Plumpton Rd

K5
1 Kestrel Cl
2 Matthews Cl

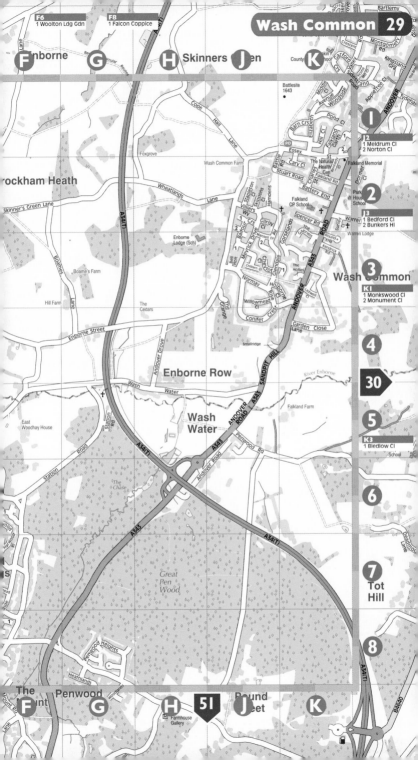

F6
1 Woolton Ldg Gdn

F8
1 Falcon Coppice

F Enborne   **G**   **H** Skinners **J** en   **K**

County School

Battlesite 1643

Falkland Memorial

Brockham Heath

I

J2
1 Meldrum Cl
2 Norton Cl

Wash Common Farm

Essex
Cary Cl
Stuart Road
Battery End

Park House School

2

J3
1 Bedford Cl
2 Bunkers Hl

Warren Lodge

Foxgrove

Wheatlands Lane

Skinner's Green Lane

Enborne Lodge (Sch)

Villiers Wy
Stepleton
Stiggons Rd
Hamdens
Gilroy Cl
Spencer Rd
Corselands
Mansell Rd

3 Wash Common

K1
1 Monkswood Cl
2 Monument Cl

Boame's Farm

Hill Farm

The Cedars

Enborne Street

Normay
Holbern
Willowmead
Conifer Cres

The Grange

Smallridge

Garden Close

4

30

Boame's Lane

Enborne Row

River Enborne

Falkland Farm

5

K3
1 Bledlow Cl

School

East Woodhay House

Wash Water
Wash Water

Station Rd

ANDOVER ROAD
SANDPIT HILL
Penwood Rd

6

The Chase

Great Pen Wood

Penwood Heights

7 Tot Hill

8

F The int   **G** Penwood   **H**   51   **J** ound eet   **K**

Farmhouse Gallery

Heathlands

F1
1 Marchant Cl
2 Pritchard Cl

Pigeon's Farm

F **G** **H** **25** **J** **K**

Greydon... se Road

Your... Crs

Farm Rd

Rose Road

Wormleave Rd 1 1 2
Pigeons

Bowdown House

Golf Course

Bury's Bank

Bury's Bank Road

I

The Round House

Bury's Bank Road

2

Greenham Common
Airfield (disused)

Seventh St
Sixth St
Fifth St

Ministry Road

Watermill Theatre

Third Street
Third St

Birchwood...
Windsborough...

First St

3
dfinch
Bottom

Foxhold

Second Street
Second

New Greenham Park
Leisure Cen

A339(T)

Thornford Road

4

River Enborne

Adbury House

Aldern
Bridge House

Sydmonton
Common

**Bishop's
Green**

Knightsbridge
House

32

5

Knight... Dr

Ash Rd
Elm Rd
Willow Rd

Eagle Road

Brooksfield

Hyde Lane

6

A339(T)

Adbury Farm

Headley Stud

7

North
Sydmonton House

North
Ecchinswell Farm

8

Frith

F **G** **H** **53** **J** **K**

**Brock's
Green**

Hyde
Farm

Whitehouse Farm

32

A   B   C   D   E

Thatcham Town
Football
B5
1 Thornfield

River Kennet

I

The
Round House

Bury's Bank Road

2

Crookham
House

Crookham
Common

3

**Goldfinch
Bottom**

RG19

Thornford Road

Foxhold

4

Ford Road

31

Folly Farm

Knightsbridge
House

5

Knightsbridge
Dr

Thornford Road

Mill
Green

Millgreen Lane

6

A339(T)

PO   Ashford Hill Road

7

Headley Stud

Headley

Common Road

Hillhouse Lane

8

Cheam Hawtreys
School

Galley
Lane

Durbidges

Hillhouse La

Hyde
Farm

Catt's
Place

**Plastow
Gr**

A   B   **54**   C   D   E

Waits Farm

1 grid square represents 500 metres

K2
1 Bannister Pl

F G H J K

Brimpton
Mill

Manor   Lane

Manor Farm

Brimpton Road

I

Brimpton

Stone House

Church Lane

PO

The
Business

Brimpton
School

Einborne Way 1

2

Crookham

Hyde End Lane

Little
Park House

3

Oak
Cott

Hyde
End

4

West Berkshire
Hampshire County

34

River Enborne

5

Goose
Hill

Riddings Farm

Riddings Lane

Woodhouse Lane

Hockford

Woodhouse Farm

6

Ashford Hill Road

Old
Lane

B3051

7

Old Farm

Ashford Hill

Chapel La

Ashford
Hill Primary
School

Tucker's
Hill Stud

Lane

sclere
dlands

Farm

The Holt

8

Holt Cottages

F G H 55 J K

Fair Oak

34

A B C D E

River Enborne

1

Manor Farm

Wasing Lower Farm

Wasing Lane

rimpton

2

The Business Centre

Shalford Farm

Wasing Park

Wasing

Brimpton School

3

Wasing Farm

4

Boot Farm

Back Lane

33

Wasing Wood

5

Blacknest Farm

Hockford Lane

6

Brimpton Common

B3051

B3051

7

The Hurst Community School

Long Gr

Inhurst House School

Woodbarn

Falcon Wy

Portway

Haughurst Hill

Brimpton Road

Inhurst Lane

Stokes Lane

Haughurst Hill

Heathrow Copse

Baughurst Road

8

The Hurst

Holt Cottages

Wolverton Road

Inhurst

ir Oak

A B

56

C D E

Hurst Farm

Wolverton Road

Axmansford

Baughurst

J2
1 Woodside Cl

Four Houses
Corner

Longmoor

Padworth Road
Reading Road

Berkshire Circular Routes

Brewery Common

Manhes Farm

Windmill

Victoria Road

Groves

The Cl's

King Street

Hammonds Heath

Road

The Bevers

Mortimer Surg

Briarlea Rd

Pitfield

Croft

Stephens

Stephens Rd

Steph Close

Firs

St Ch

Birchland Cl

Ravensworth Cl

Sweetzer Piece

Laneswood

West End Road

Stanmore Gdns

Loves Wood

St Mary's Rd

St John's Rd

Garth Rd

St Johns School

Berkshire Circular Routes

Mortimer

The Orchard Road

The Avenue

Street Lane

Mortimer Lodge

The Avenue

The Avenue

West End Farm

Mortimer West End

Simms Farm Lane

Turk's Lane

Simms Stud Farm

Drury Lane

Berkshire Circular Routes

38

Brocas Lands Farm

Sheepgrove Farm

Park Lane

Wall Lane

Berkshire Circular Routes

Church Lane

North Copse

Clappers Farm Rd

Brickledon's Farm

Lavell's Farm

Lavell's

59

Lower Farm

Bramley Road

Three Ashes

I grid square represents 500 metres

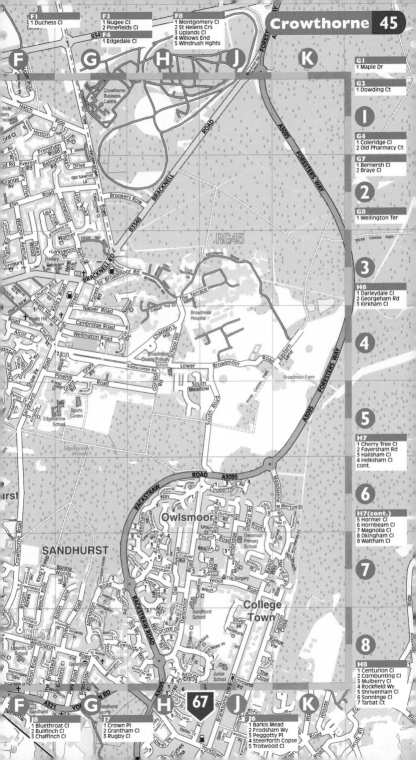

F1
L 1 Duchess Cl

F3
1 Nugee Ct
2 Pinefields Cl

F4
1 Edgedale Cl

F8
1 Montgomery Cl
2 St Helens Crs
3 Uplands Cl
4 Willows End
5 Windrush Hghts

G1
1 Maple Dr

G2
1 Dowding Ct

G4
1 Coleridge Cl
2 Old Pharmacy Ct

G7
1 Bernersh Cl
2 Braye Cl

G8
1 Wellington Ter

H6
1 Darleydale Cl
2 Georgeham Rd
3 Kirkham Cl

H7
1 Cherry Tree Cl
2 Faversham Rd
3 Hailsham Cl
4 Helksham Cl
cont.

H7(cont.)
5 Hormer Cl
6 Hornbeam Cl
7 Magnolia Cl
8 Okingham Cl
9 Waltham Cl

H8
1 Centurion Cl
2 Cornbunting Cl
3 Mulberry Cl
4 Rockfield Wy
5 Shrivenham Cl
6 Sonninge Cl
7 Tarbat Ct

J8
1 Bluethroat Cl
2 Bullfinch Cl
3 Chaffinch Cl

I7
1 Crown Pl
2 Grantham Cl
3 Rugby Cl

J8
1 Barkis Mead
2 Frodsham Wy
3 Peggotty Pl
4 Steerforth Copse
5 Trotwood Cl

Town Farm

Road

Downs Lane

Buttermere

Hearn Lane

Grange Farm

Church Lane

White Farm

Manor Farm

Ballyack House

Buttermere Wood

Rockmoor Down

Combe Wood

Wiltshire County

Hampshire County

Trent Way

Rockmoor Lane

Winterside Farm

Littledown

Vernham Street

Box Farm

Manor House

PO

Manor Far

I

2

3

4

48

5

6

7

8

F G H J K

F G H 71 J K

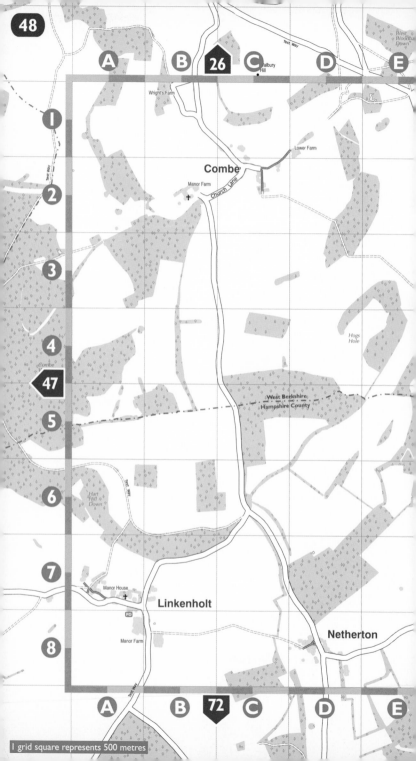

F **G** **H** **27** **J** **K**

East Woodhay

St Martins East Woodhay
College of Education
Primary School

Bar
Cro

I

Stargrove

2

Hampshire County
West Berkshire

Wayfarer's Walk

Wayfarer's
Walk

3

Eastwick

Wayfarer's Walk

4

50

5

Wayfarer's Walk

6

7

Faccombe

Curzon
Street Farm

Privet
Copse

8

F **G** **H** **73** **J** **K**

Steeles Farm

50

A B **28** C D E

Fullers Lane Malverleys

Copse Farm

Doctors Surgery

St Thomas Infant School

Woolton Hill

Wo Hill Jun

Comber Close

Church Lane

I St Martins East Woodhay College of Education Primary School

Barn Croft

Stargrove

East End

Hotel

Cro V

2

Tower House

3

Jones' Farm

Hollington Lane

4 Hollington Lane

Hollington

V

Kinghams Farm

Hollington Lane

Hollington Lane

49

Highclere Street

5

Hollington Cross

PH

6

Zell House Farm

Brandier Views

7

Coles Wood

Privet Copse

Wayfarer's Walk

8

Manor Farm

Three Legs House

Dark Cross Lane

Cross Lane

HILL A343

A B **74** C D E

PO

Ashmansworth

Steeles Farm

I grid square represents 500 metres

A **B** **30** **C** **D** **E**

Heatherwold

Earlstone Common

Burghclere

The Clere Secondary School

Palmer's Hill House

1

Breedmoor Plantation

Church Lane

St Michaels School

Burghclere CP School

Norman Farm

Sandham Memorial Chapel (NT)

2

Pound Lane

Harts Lane

Well Street

Budd's Farm

Scring Lane

3

West Street

Wellhouse Farm

temple

Earlstone Manor

4

West Street

Ridgemoor Farm

Well Street

51

itway

A34(T)

5

Duncroft Farm

6

White Hill

7

Wergs Farm

8

Old Burghclere

Ivory Farm

A **B** **76** **C** **D** **E**

1 grid square represents 500 metres

F G H **31** J K

Brock's Green

North Ecchinswell Farm

Hyde Farm

Frith Copse

Whitehouse Farm

Hyde Lane

Kisby's Farm

Woodside Farm

Cowhouse Farm

✝

Mill Lane

54

Oakfields Close

White Hill

Ecchinswell

rtobury Farm

Watership Farm

Nuthanger Farm

monton Court

Fossicks

monton

Watership Down

F G **77** J K

1 2 3 4 54 5 6 7 8

A   B   32   C   D   E

Plastow
Green

1

Hyde
Farm

Waits Farm

Strattons

2

Kisby's Farm

Pitchorn Farm

Upper
House Farm

3

Hall's Farm

Union Lane

Harridens Farm

4

Stanton's Farm

53

Frobury Farm

NEWBURY ROAD

Union Lane

5

Hardys Fld
Keeps
Mead
Wellington
Meadow
Frogs
Hole

The Lines

Strokins Rd

Greenlands
Road

Coppice Road

ECCHINSWELL ROAD

The Paddock
Canon's Court

North Street

George St

Kingsclere
Health
Centre

Primary
School

B3051

6

Fox's Ln

Swan St

Popes Hill

King John
Road

Love
Lane

Basingstoke

Higmans

Hook
Road

Queens
Road

GEORGE ST

7

Bear Hil

KINGSCLERE

Hollowshot Lane

CHESTER ROAD

8

Park House Stables

A   B   78   C   D   E

1 grid square represents 500 metres

F
G
H
33
J
K

sclere
ds

The Holt

Holt Cottag

1

Farm

Fair Oak

LITTLE KNOWLE HILL

Wheat Hold

2

B3051

Dairy
House Farm

3

Wolverton Road

Frith Farm

Chapel
Lane

4

Holt Lane

56

Wolvert
Comm

Frith Common
Farm

Sandford
Woods

Wolverton
Wood

5

Golf
Course

Sandford Springs
Golf Club

Wolverton Road

Church Lane

6

Crabs Hill

Wolverton House

Ramsdell Road

Ramsdell Road

7

Rector Lane

The Old
House

Wolverton Lane

Wolverton

8

Foscol Farm

A339(T)

Hollington Lane

F
G
H
79
J
K

Plantation Farm

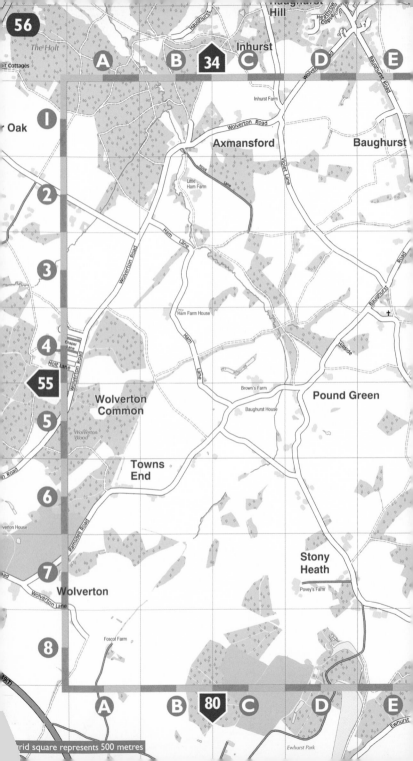

H1
1 Abbottswood Cl
2 Candover Cl
3 Cheriton Cl
4 Herriard Wy
5 Monks Wood Crs

H2
1 Crookham Cl

Gorselands

F G H 35 J K

Hamble Drive

The Orchard

Brook Green Road

Bowmon Road

Junior School

Infant School
Morland Surgery

New Road

Hinton Close

New Road

Fullerton

Warblington Close

North View Road

Swedish Houses

Vine Tree Close

I

J1
1 Christy Ct
2 Finch Cl
3 Titchfield Cl

New Road

Lane

Church

Brook

Hawley House

TADLEY

Graveley Close

The Green

Rectory Close

Tadley C E School

Manse La

Malthouse Lane

Cedar

Forest Lane

Mariners Close

2

Church Rd

Church

Lane

Brook

Church Brook Farm

Skate's Lane

Skate's Farm

Mariner's Copse

3

Church Road

Kimbers La

A340 ALDERMASTON RD

4

Green La

Browninghill Green

58 amber en

A340 ALDERMASTON ROAD

5

Court Corner

Wyeford Farm

6

Hollybush Lane

Old Vine Lane

West Heath

Ramsdell Road

Pamber End

7

The Priory Primary School

Priory Farm

8

White Hart Lane

Sherborne Road

Charter Alley

Tubb's

Bear's Prightle

Rawlins Farm

A340

Monk

Sherborne Road

Skyer's Farm

F G H 81 J K

RG26

Dasn Lane

Ramsdell

J5
1 Pheaben's Fld

K5
1 Jibbs Meadow
2 Longbridge Rd

F G H 37 J K

North Copse
Clappers Farm Rd
Kledon's Farm
Lavell's Farm
Lavell's

I

Lower Farm
Bramley Road

Three Ashes

2

Haines Farm

Barefoot House

3

Stratfield Saye

here Green

Minchens Lane

Holly Cross

Bramley Lane

Oliver's Lane

4

Oliver's Farm

Clift Surgery

Bramley

Bramley C of E Primary School
Meitner Cl
Tottenham Cl
Browns Cl
Moat Close
Bramley Lane
Bromelia Close
PO
Osler Cl

60

Strawberry Fields

The Street

Silchester Road

Church Lane

Bramley Station
Ringhall Gdns
Ellen Gdns
Church Cl
Coopers Lane
Shortfield Road
Longbridge Rd

Coopers Ct
The Smithy
Farriers Cl
Doct Cl

5

Middle Farm
Baker's Reserve Cl

Bramley Corner

Bram

End
Bramley Green
Forge
German

6

The Maltings

Locksbridge Lane

Bow Brook

7

Watford Copse

Vyne Road

Baker's Farm

8

Vyne Lodge Farm

F G H 83 J K

Cufaude

Upper Cufaude Farm

F G H 39 J K

I
2
3
4
62
5
6
7
8

tfield
e

Green Lane

Kings Farm

Stratfield
Saye

ROAD

BASINGSTOKE

A River Loddon

Park
Pitham
Copse

Lower
Pitham

Hotel
PH

A33

Lawn Farm

Daneshill
School

Stratfield
Turgis

shery

Turgis
Green

A33

Bylands Farm

Sheldons Farm

Spanish
Green

arm

Hartley House

Chandlers
Green

Hartley Lane

Hartley
Wespall

River Loddon

Rotherwick Lane

Mill Lane

Rotherwick

Lane

Lodd Lane

F G H 85 J K

Lance Levy Farm

Mill Farm

Mill
Lane

Lyde Green

J2
1 Honeysuckle Cl
2 Tresham Crs

K1
1 Fareham Dr

Eversley
Centre

F G H 43 J K

Eversley Cricket Club.

Eversley Cross

Canberra Close

Blaire Pk

Coombe Rd

Mougharn La

Castles Path

Sherlock Lea

Yeomans

New Road

Brooklands

Three Castles Path

Crosby Tower Gdns

READING ROAD

Vicarage

I

K2
1 Falcon Wy
2 Mallard Wy
3 Raven Cl
4 Turnstone End
5 Wren Cl

2

K3
1 Badgers Holt

Yateley School

3

K4
1 Brocklands
2 Byron Cl

Up Green

COOPER'S HILL

MARSH LANE

B3016

Firgrove Manor

Firgrove Road

Rokes Pl

Dunsmore Gdns

Oldcorne Hollow

Huddington Gld

Kits Croft

Firgromorton Road

Catesby Gdns

Celandine Ct

Firgrove

Bramling

Partridge Av

Westfield County Junior School

Monteagle Lane

Hilltop Vw

Selwyn

Hardy

Herriot Court

Avenue

Wordsworth

Stookes Way

Harvest Close

Benneman Walk

Little Vigo

Keats

Blackbushe Airport

Eversley Common

4

66

5

A30

6

Hartford

A327

7

West Valley Farm

B3013

Blackbushes Road

Ivyhoe Hill

Yateley Heath Wood

8

Blackbushe Farm

1 grid square represents 500 metres

F1 1 Gainsborough Cl
F3 1 Crawley Wood Cl
F6 1 Mulgrave Rd

High Curley

F7
1 Broughton Ms
2 Kilmartin Gdns
3 Stamford Av

F8
1 Oldbury Cl
2 Petworth Cl

G1
1 Silverwood Dr

G3
1 Ardrossan Av
2 Southcote Dr

H1
1 Darracott Cl

H4
1 Amber Hl
2 Bentley Copse

J1
1 Consort Dr
2 Curtis Cl

J3
1 Augustus Gdns

J4
1 Pollard Gv
2 Redmayne

K6
1 Marshall Cl
2 Myers Wy

K5
1 Gosnell Cl

K3
1 Brackenwood
2 Englesfield
3 Greenholme

J5
1 Edgemoor Rd
2 Haslemere Cl
3 Paterson Cl

Heatherside

Frimley Ridge

Frimley

Frim Green

F G H **47** J K

Box Farm

I

Manor Farm

Vernham Street

Tort Way

Vernham Dean

The Dell

PO

Back Lane

Earlstone Cl

Hatchbury Lane

Shepherds Rise

Blights Hill

School Cl

Vernham Dean School

Vernham Manor

2

3

Wilster Copse

Ankers Farm

Upton Manor

4

Tonholt Lane

72

Upton

5

Ambley Farm

6

Rushmore Down

7

8

ft Lane

Locke's Drove

Whistler's Farm

Pill Heath Farm

F G H 51 J K

Ivory Farm

I

Wayfarer's Walk

Highclere Stud

rotto
opse

262
▲
Beacon
Hill

2

Upper
Woodcott
Down

3

Wayfarer's Walk

4

76

Lower
Woodcott
Down

Hook
Copse

5

oodcott

6

A34/11

Lower Woodcott Farm

7

Woodcott House

8 Litchfiel

Buckets Down Farm

Dunley

Angl
Cops

A B **56** C D E

I

2

3

4

79

5

6

7

8

Foscot Farm

Ewhurst Park

Home Farm

Ewhurst House

Skyer's Wood

Lloyd's Lane

Pitt Hall Fm

Folly Dairy

Balstone Farm

Ibworth

Upper Wootton

Hook Lane

Tangier

A B **106** C D E

Shear Down Farm

I grid square represents 500 metres

F6
1 Carpenter's Dwn

F8
1 Lansley Rd
2 Normanton Rd
3 Stratfield Rd

F **G** **H** **59** **J** **K**

Cufaude

Upper Cufaude Farm

Vyne Lodge Farm

Baker's Farm

Cufaude Lane

I

G6
1 Falkland Rd
2 Montserrat Pl
3 Tasmania Cl

2

G8
1 Myland Cl

Razor's Farm

Vyne Farm

Mary's Lane

3

J5
1 Aghemund Cl
2 Southlands

Crockford Lane

Tree Way

Belvedere Gdns

Thornhill

Saffron

Petty's

Reno

Maybrook

Achilles

4

Juniper

Mongers Piece

Bowman Rd

84

Thornhill

Carpenters Down Wood

Chineham
Whitewood
Sorrel's Close

Kings Pightle Way

Matlock

5

J6
1 Great Oaks Cha
2 Longacre Ri
3 Minden Cl

Jersey Cl
Guernse

Down

Tasmania
Bermuda
Dominica

Falkland

Angmans
Fadstine
Pitcairn

Hammer Road

Mayflower Close
Talmey Cl

Great Oaks Chase

The New
Chineham Surg

Reading Rd

Clere Gdns

6

K4
1 Greenwood Dr
2 Parkwood Cl
3 Renown Wy

Tobago
Malta
Close

Ascension

Shetland

Marnel Infant &
Junior Schools

Faroe

Popley
Way

Glade Cl

Hartswood

Minden Close

Stroud Cl

Onslow Cl

Superstore

A33

Pyotts Court

7

K5
1 Birchwood
2 Larchwood
3 Martins Wd
4 Thurnwood

Pershore
Road

Pershore
Rd

John Hunt
of Everest
Community
School

Popley

Shakespeare
Dryden
Keats

Byron

Lawrence

Chaucer

Longfellow
Parade Clinic

Doctors' Surgery

Chineham Pk Ct

Rutherford
Rd

Bilton
Industrial Estate

Bilton Industrial
Est

Binfields Cl

Binfields

Lutyens
Close

Marshcourt

Badger's Bank

Heron
Dr

Daneshill

8

K5

Ivar Gdns

Pyo

Binfields

39 **RINGWAY NORTH**

Oakridge Rd

Shakespear

Primary
School

A33 READING ROAD

Basingstoke & Deane
Borough Council

Danesbill

Badger's Bank

Church Grange

Little Basing

Little Fallow

East
Barn Road

Oakridge

Dove
House
School

Gower

Arliott Drive

James Close

Lefroy
Av

Baynard

Silvester

Martin
Free
Pantile

K8
1 Bracken Bank
2 Clover Fld
3 Crofters Meadow
4 Dragonfly Dr

Daneshill
Ind Estate
Danes
Indust

K6
1 Hazeldene
2 Rememb'ce Gdn
3 St Joseph's Crs
4 Wallins Copse

Upfallow
Little Basing

PH

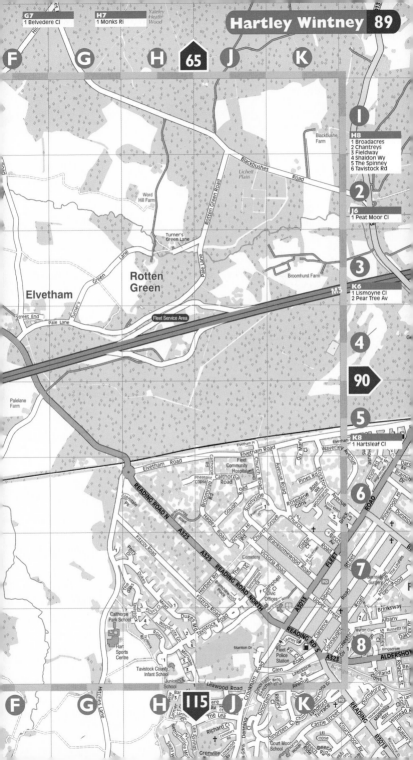

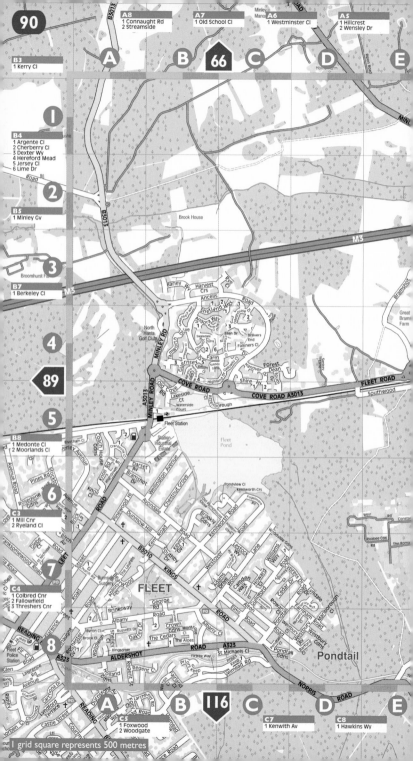

F4
1 Marjoram Cl

G3
1 Baywood Cl
2 Cherry Tree Cl
3 Kenilworth Rd
4 Nutmeg Ct
5 Pinewood Crs
6 Purmerend Cl

G4
1 Coriander Cl
2 Pyestock Crs

G5
1 Ash Tree Cl
2 Grenadiers Wy
3 The Pathfinders
4 Regiment Cl
5 Rifle Wy
6 Stanley Dr
7 Whitebeams Gdn
8 Yew Tree Cl

H3
1 Shakespeare Gdn
2 Twelve Acre Crs

I4
1 Westglade
2 Woodcot Gdns

H5
1 Cornelia Cl
2 Lauderdale
3 Lodsworth
4 Nevada Cl
5 Palmerston Cl
6 Rydal Cl
7 Tweedsmuir Cl

I1
1 Cairngorm Pl
2 Fintry Pl
3 Snowdon Rd

J5
1 Ferndown Gdns
2 Kendal Cl
3 Langdale Cl

J5
1 Primrose Gdns
2 Windermere Cl

J6
1 Heather Gdns

K5
1 Maple Leaf Cl
2 St Christoph'rs Pl
3 Wilson Rd

K4
1 Cottage Gdns
2 Cranleigh Ct

K1
1 Pegasus Rd

Cove

West Heath

Rafborough

Southwood

Farnborough Airport

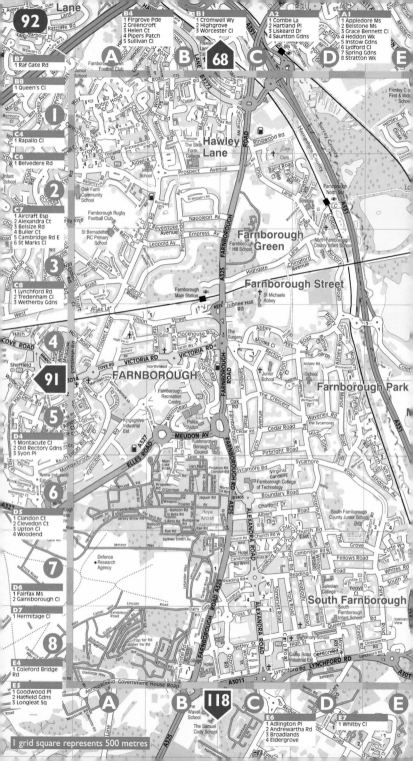

F
G
H
71
J
K

I

2

3

4

Doles Farm
98

5

6

7

8

Locke's Drove

Whistler's Farm

Pill
Heath Farm

Tangley
Farm

*Blagden
Copse*

Blagden House

The Avenue
Wildhern

Plough Farm

Hatherden
Manor

Hungerford Lane

The
Close

Hatherden
House

Hungerford Lane

Cemetery

Hatherden C of E
Primary School

Hatchet Lane

Hatherden

Goddards Farm

Pigeon
House Farm

Charlton Down
Farm

A   B   72   C   D   E

D8
1 Ridges Cl

C8
1 Greenfields

Ke's Drove

Pill
Heath Farm

Windmill Lane

Windmills

Horseshoe Lane

River Swift

Dine Close

Beacon Drove

CRUX

1

2

3

4

97

5

6

7

8

Blagden
Copse

Doles Farm

A343 NEWBURY ROAD

Boorne
Park

Rag's
Copse

dhern

Plough Farm

Green Drove

Charlton Down
Farm

Little
London

Upper
Enham

MacCullum Road

Victoria Court

Kings Road

Dunhills Lane

Malt

A   B   126   C   D   E

Enham Alamein

Newbury Road

NE

Lancaster Rd

Alamein Rd

Tobruk
Close

Knightsbridge

Smannell & Enham
Primary School

1 grid square represents 500 metres

The Dene

ourne

F G H 73 J K

I
2
3
4
100
5
6
7
8

B3048

STOKE LANE

Bourne Rivulet

Prior's Farm

Slade Bottom Farm

B3048

Long Cholderton

Stoke

Stokehill Farm

Stoke Hill

Gangbridge Lane

Oak Tree Farm

Test Way

Upper Wyke

Stoke Road

Hackwood Copse

Middle Wyke Farm

Finkley Road

Test Way

F G H 127 J K

100

74

99

128

A B C D E

1

2

3

4

5

6

7

8

Binley

Wadwick

Slade Bottom Farm

Elm Farm

Binley Bottom

Cold Harbour

Wadwick Bottom

Wakeswood

Cangbridge Lane

Swampton

Test Way

Bagley Hill

Spring Hill

School Road

Bourne Road

Edbury Road

Stevens Green

St Mary Bourne

Bourne Court

PO

PH

Village School

Bourne
Meadow

Lane

Test Way

Derry Down
Health Clinic

South View
Ter

B3048

Bailey

Road

Middle
Wyke Farm

Test Way

Derrydown
Farm

B3048

B3048

Road

1 grid square represents 500 metres

Ashfield

A   B   76   C   D   E

Wolnley Copse

1

2

Angledown Copse

3   Clap Gate

Twinley Manor

4

101

5   Cole Henley Manor Farm

Cole Henley

6

RG28

Wooldings Farm

7   The Orchards

Harroway   Newbury Road

8   Down Farm

Harroway

A   B   130 m   C   D   E

Priory Lane

A34(T)   Newbury Road   Barrow Hill   Larks

F G H **77** J K

1

2

3

4

104

5

6

7

8

Ridgeway Farm

Willesley Warren Farm

Whitnal

New Barn

Court Drove

Hill Meadow

Primary School

Court Farm

Longlands Court
Mill Lane
Glebe Meadow
Church Roa
Overt Galle

Lynch

The Lynch
Silk Mill
Southington
Close
Southington Close
White Hart Gallery
Red Lion Lane
Bridge St
HIGH ST

F G H **131** J K

Home Farm

Laverstoke Ho

Sou**K**ngton

B3400

TOTTEN HILL

Dellands Lane

Oak Close

Poultons
Road
bellands
Charlesborough
Close

Caesar's
Belt

F G H 79 J K

Warrener's Walk

Freemantle Farm

1

Hay Wood

White Lane

2

Warrener's Walk

Frith Wood

3

Great Deane Wood

Summer Down Lane

4

Ashe Warren Ho

Little Deane Wood

106

Warrener's Walk

5

Deane Down Farm

Harrow Way

N Down Lane

Clarken Green

6

C O

RECT

ANDOVER ROAD

7

Deane

ANDOVER ROAD P11

8

33400

Cheesedown Farm

Ashe Park

F G H 133 J K

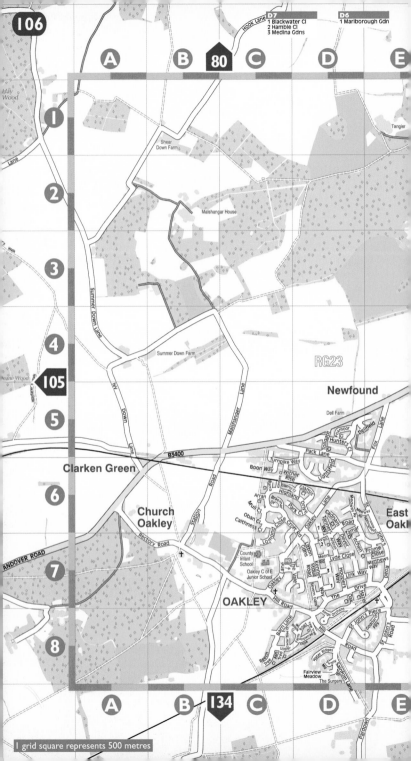

106

80

134

105

A B C D E

RG23

Hay Wood

Lane

Shear Down Farm

Malshanger House

Summer Down Lane

Summer Down Farm

Ivy Down Lane

Malshanger Lane

Westcroft Way

Pestre Wood

Newfound

Dell Farm

Smoor

Dellfield

Hunters

Fox Lane

Pack Lane

Tollgate

Longfield

Turnpike Way

Boon Way

Wither Rise

Highland

Dominie

Park Close

B3400

Clarken Green

Church Oakley

Station Road

Rectory Road

ANDOVER ROAD

Arran

Mull Cl

Oban Cl

Caithness Cl

Loweswater

Park Way

Croft Gdns

Andover Road

County Infant School

Oakley C of E Junior School

OAKLEY

Meon

Lyde Close

Kennet Road

Avon Cl

Tamar Way

Itchen

Frome Close

Matthews Way

East Oakl

Barn Lane

Beech Tree

Upper

Deer Ridges

Fairview Meadow

The Surgery

Saltgrun Lane

St John's Piece

St John's Road

Pardown

The Drive

Hill Road

The Orchard

Tangier

1 grid square represents 500 metres

F1
1 Marshall Gdns
2 Middleton Gdns
3 Normanton Rd
4 St Thomas' Cl
F4
1 Anchor Yd
F5
1 Montague Pl
G1
1 Cowdrey Cl
G2
1 Gordon Cl
G3
1 St Mary's Ct
G5
1 Camrose Wy
2 Chesterfield Rd
3 Howard Rd
H3
1 Buckby La
2 The Butty
3 Colne Wy
4 Duddon Wy
5 Hamble Ct
6 Medway Ct
7 Ribble Wy
8 Roding Cl
9 Rothay Ct
10 Severn Wy
11 Thames Ct
12 Trent Wy
13 Weysprings Cl
K1
1 Blackberry Wk
2 Whitehead Cl
83
5
110
137
Oakridge
Daneshill
Eastrop
Black Dam
Basingstoke Station
Basingstoke & Deane Borough Council
Daneshill Ind Estate
Daneshill Industrial Estate
Daneshill East Industrial Estate
Hassocks Wood Industrial Est
Loddon Business Cen
The Hampshire Clinic
The AA - Fanum House
Police Station
Basingstoke County Court
The Malls/The Walks Shopping Cen
Basingstoke Sports Cen
EASTROP ROUNDABOUT
A3010 CHURCHILL WAY EAST
RINGWAY EAST
RINGWAY SOUTH
A339
A30
M3
Junction 6
Surrey Hants Borders NHS Trust
The Business Cen
Magistrates Court
Haymarket Theatre
Harriet Costello School
Civic Offices
Basingstoke & Deane Borough Council Offices
War Memorial Park
John Arlott Pavilion
HACKWOOD ROAD ROUNDABOUT
Hampshire County Council
Deane's Almhouses
Beaconsfield Rd Primary School
Dove House School
Phoenix Park Terrace
Cowdrey Hts
Dicken's Lane Plantation
Home Farm
Audleys Wood
Hackwood House
Hackwood Park
FARLEIGH ROAD
B3046
HACKWOOD RD
RG21

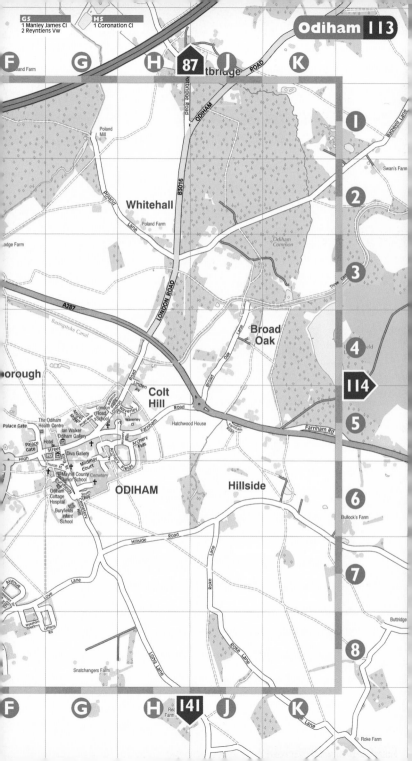

GS
1 Manley James Cl
2 Reyntiens Vw

HS
1 Coronation Cl

F G H **87** tbridge J K

I 1

Swan's Farm

Poland Mill

2 2

B3016

Whitehall

Poland Lane

Poland Farm

Odiham Common

Lodge Farm

3 3

A287

Basingstoke Canal

LONDON ROAD

Broad Oak

4 4

orough

Linden Av

Colt Hill

114

Road

Broad Oak Lane

The Odiham Health Centre

Ian Walker

Odiham Gallery

Waverley Cl

Road

Farnham

Hatchwood House

Farnham Rd

5 5

Palace Gate

Hotel

London Road School

High Street

Church St

Diva Gallery

Mildmay Court

Archery Flds

Archery Fields

Farnham Road

Palace Gate

Mayhill County School

Buryfields Junior School

ODIHAM

Hillside

6 6

Odiham Cottage Hospital

Buryfields Infant School

Cemetery

South Road

Cemetery Hill

Bullock's Farm

Hillside Road

7 7

Avenue

Love Lane

Roke Lane

Wrabham Colett

LaHarry's Rd

Buttridge

8 8

Long Lane

Roke Lane

Snatchangers Farm

Roke Farm

F G H **141** J K

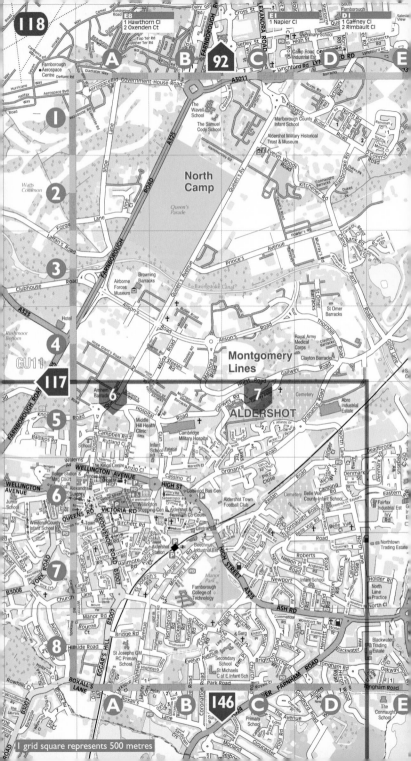

F2
1 Woodcock Cl

F4
1 Canons Cl
2 Deans Cl

I

G1
1 Forest Dr

2

G2
1 Gisbourne Cl
2 Pheasant Cl
3 Sycamore Cl

3

K1
1 Brisbane Cl
2 Sydney Cl

4

122

5

6

7

8

Perham Down

NORTH TIDWORTH

uth Tidworth

LUDGERSHALL ROAD

A3026

Wylye

Road

Clarendon
County Junior
& Infant School

ce Rd

Tidworth
Health
Centre

Group
Practice

tion Road

down Terrace

Plantation
Rd

rse Hill Road

Church Lane

hworton

Ash
Cl

Kestrel

Forest
Cl

Martin

Bourne

Kennet

Napier

Auckland Cl

Lambdown Terrace

Lamsdown
Terrace

Kettlemead

Woodham Cl

Somme

Upnor
Cl

Adelaide Cl

Benin Terrace Rd

Appleshaw
Way

Fyfield
Way

Downsview
Way

Lamb
Down

Wiltshire County
Hampshire

Ashdown Copse

Wiltshire County
Hampshire County

Old Coach Road

F G H **149** J K

Snoddington

Snoddington Down Farm

A B **94** C D E

Somme

Wouldham Road

1
Manor Close

Avebury Close

2 1

Fyfield Way
Benbow
Chilton
Lambay Down

2

Shoddesden Lane

South Park

Andover Lane

Great Shoddesden

Wiltshire County
Hampshire County

Newdown Copse

3

Deacon Road

4

121

Kimpton Down Farm

Deacon Rd

Down Road

Cow La

Deacon Road

5

Kimpton Wood

6

Ox Drove

Down Road

Kimpton

7

Ox Drove

8

Snoddington Road

Thruxton Aerodrome and Motor Racing Circuit

A B **150** C D E

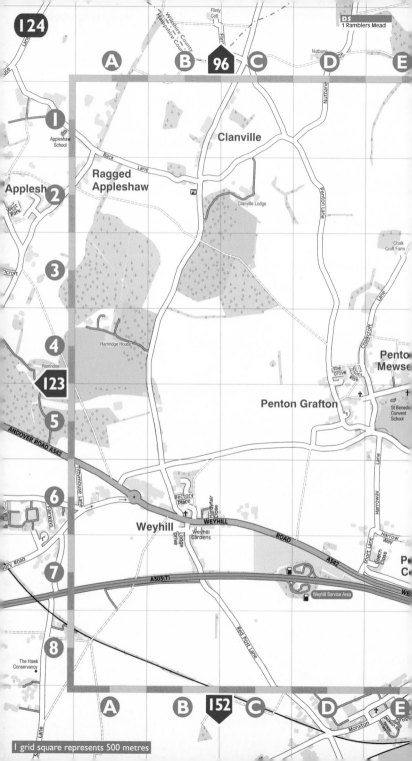

Andover 125

SP11

H5
1 Augustine Wy
2 Barton Cl
3 Brancaster Av
4 Ethelbert Dr
5 Hengest Cl
6 Home Farm Gdns

H6
1 Kimberley Cl

Charlton Down Farm

I6
1 The Green

I7
1 Silver Birch Rd
2 Thistledown Cl

Knights Enham

I8
1 Lodge Cl

Manor Fan

K4
1 Marsum Cl

K5
1 Hamburg Cl
2 Lingen Cl
3 Minden Cl
4 Verden Wy

K6
1 Hattem Pl

K8
1 The Crossways
2 Saor Ms

K7
1 Lancaster Cl
2 Lowry Ct

Penton Copses

Cemetery

New Street Football Club

Foxcotte

Foxcotte Lane

Andover Football Club West Portway

Charlton

CHURCHILL WAY WEST

War Memorial Hospital

Harrow Way Community School

Charlton Hill Surgery

Charlton Healthy Centre

Andover Stn

WEYHILL

Portway County Infants and Junior Schools

John Hanson Community School

St John the Baptist RC Primary School

WESTERN RD

Balksbury

1 grid square represents 500 metres

A   B   100   C   D   E

South Vw Ter

B3048

Middle
Wyke Farm

Road

Derrydown
Farm

1

Chapmansford Farm

Lower
Wyke Farm

2

Harroway

3

Apsley Farm

Bourne Wood

4

127

Faulkner's
Down Farm

5

The
Common

Harewood

6

Fox
Cottages

B3400

7

Budgett Farm

8

Tracy's
Dell

A   B   156   C   D   E

F G H J K

105

Andover Road PH

Cheesedown Farm

Ashe Park

1

2
Wayfarer's Walk

3

Steventon

4
Stubb's Copse

Basset's Farm

134

5
Village Farm

West Wood

6

North

Waltham
Lane
Manor Farm

North Waltham School

Folly Farm

7
Yew Tree Lane

Coldharbour

Steventon Warren Farm

8
PH

161

A30

H1
1 Brambling Cl
2 Pintail Cl

J1
1 Berewyk Cl
2 Bunting Ms
3 Sunflower Cl

K1
1 Chantry Ms
2 Fayrewood Cha
3 Matilda Dr
4 Paxton Cl
5 Sandbanks Dr
6 Westminster Cl
7 Wights Wk

K2
1 Petworth Cl

K3
1 Burrowfields
2 Grosvenor Cl

Hatch Warren

Hatch Warren
Retail Park

Hatch
Warren
Surgery

St Marks
Primary
School

Hatch Warren
Primary School

Kempshott County
Infant School

Kempshott County
Junior School

Hatch Warren
County Junior
School

Hatch Warren
County
Infant School

Golf
Course

Golf
Course

Industrial
Estate

Kennel Farm

Manor Farm

Inwood
Copse

Farleigh Lane

Beggarwood Lane

Nutley Lane

Clump Farm

Dummer

Club House

Club House

Gallery

Goble
Hole

Nutley
Wood

RG25

WINCHESTER ROAD

A30

M3

B3046

107

136

163

F G H J K I

1 2 3 4 5 6 7 8

F G H 109 J K

I

2

3 Winslade

4

138

5

6

7 Herriard

8

F G H 165 J K

Hotel

Audleys Wood

Hackwood Park

Hackwood Lane

Road

A339

Swallick Farm

Allwoods Copse

Three Castles Path

Bushywarren Lane

Church Lane

Ellisfield

Elisfield Manor

Three Castles Path

Northgate Lane

Manor Farm

Herriard Grange

142

Buttridge

A   B 114 C   D   E

Roke

1   Roke Farm

2

Newlands Farm

3   Park
                    Corner Farm

                Horsedown
                Common

Stapely Farm   Swanthorpe Farm

4

◀ 141   Thorn's Farm

Ham
Copse

5   Travers Farm

White Hill

6 PH   Montgomery

    Well   Hole Lane

7   Glade
                                    Farm
Well Lane

8

Crest
Hill Farm

A   B 170 C   D   E

1 grid square represents 500 metres

E6
1 Chantry Cl

E2
1 Ambleside Crs
2 Beck Gdns
3 Dukes Cl
4 Folly La South
5 Trinity Flds
6 Ullswater Cl

E1
1 Lawday Pl

A   B   C   D   E

Ewshot

3 Fox Way

ODIHAM ROAD

Warren
Corner

Ewshot
Hall

Hog
Hatch

Redlands

Heath Lane

Dora's Green Lane

Church Lane

Broome

Lea Farm

Warren
Corner

B3013

Old Park Lane

Heath End Road

Old Park Lane

Lawday
La

Hoghat

Dora's
Green

Upper
Old Park

Upper Old Park Lane

Fo
Hi

1

2

3

4

5

6

7

8

143

172

Clare
Park

Middle
Old Park

Middle Old Park

Knowle Farm

Old Park Lane

Lower Old
Park

Three Stiles Rd

Crondall Lane

Crondall Lane

Beavers
Hl

Beavers
Close

Dora's Green Lane

Di

Crondall Lane

Dippenhall

Larkfield Rd

Byworth
Rd

Byworth
Cl

Waynflete Lane

Hazell Rd

Chantry

Hampshire County
Surrey County

Road

Clark's Hill

Runwick Lane

Coronation

WEST STREET

Cemetery

Lane

Runwick Lane

Grovers Farm

Runwick Lane

Ridgway House

Runwick House

FARNHAM BY-F

WRECCLESHAM RD

Channel

Hotel

ROAD

River

ALTON

Lane

The
Hatches

Secondary
School

Grovebell
Industrial Est

Riverdale

Middlefield

Greenfield
Road

Lynton

A   B   C   D   E

Willey
Place

1 grid square represents 500 metres

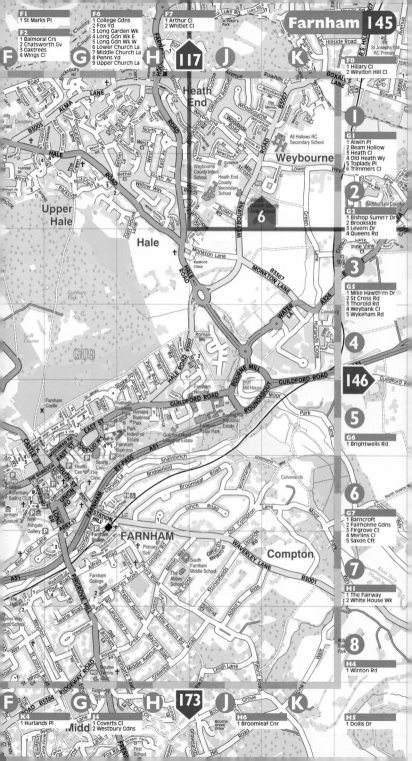

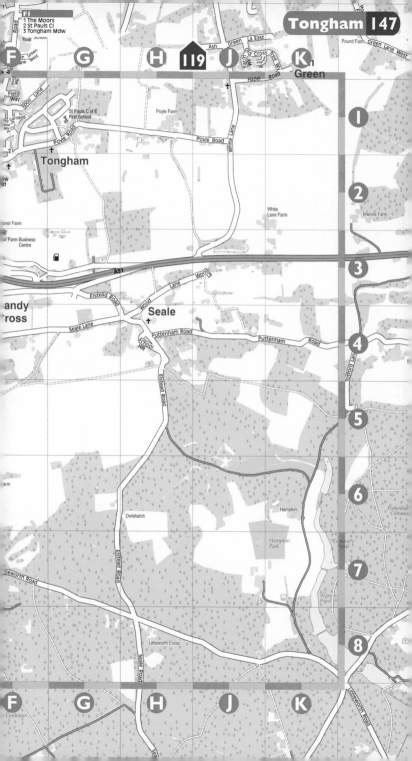

A
B
122
C
D
E

Thruxton Aerodrome and
● Motor Racing Circuit

I

2

Racedown

A303(T)

3

Lains Farm

Middlecot House

Park Lane
Etwall

4

Quarley

149

Skew Road

5

Quarley
Manor Farm

6

7

● Quarley
Hill

Grateley Drove

Grateley

The
Dell

High
Street
Hawthorne

Monxton Road

Lawrence Houses

Chapel
Lane

Grateley Junior
& Infant School

8

Portway
Farm

CHOLDERTON

ROAD

B3084

A
B
175
C
D
E

Road

Grat.
Station

Grateley
Business
Park

Station
Ap

Campbell

Road

Streetway
Road

F4
1 Gilberts Mead Cl

G1
1 Spruce Cl

F **G** **H** **125** **J** **K**

WEYHILL RD B3402

WESTERN RD

1

H1
1 Hackwood Cl

2

H2
1 Hanover Cl

3

I1
1 Chatsworth Dr
2 Durley Cl
3 Goddards Mead
4 Holmes Ct
5 Longstock Cl
6 Newtown Cl

4

154

5

J2
1 Kemmitt Wy
2 Little Copse

6

K1
1 Victoria Ct
2 Wyndham Rd

7

K2
1 The Willows

8

Anna Valley

Balksbury
Industrial
Estate

8

Upper
Clatford

Bury Hill

Goodworth
Clatford

Red Rice

Home Farm

Farleigh
School

F **G** **H** **178** **J** **K**

F G H **129** J K

East Aston

Paper Mill Farm

River Test

I

2

Larkwhistle Farm

Firgo Farm

A34(T)

Vale Farm

3

4

158

5

6

Tidbury Farm

A303(T)

7

A30

8

U B

River Dever

Roberts Road

Tidbury Common

Barton Stacey C of E Primary School

Roman Way

Green Rd

Pheasant Cl

West Road

Penrose Cl

F G H **182** J K

Bullington Lane

Colne

Way

Lower Bullington

BULLINGTON

A34(T)

New Barn Farm

Micheldever Road

Laverstoke Wood

Roundwood Farm

Freefolk Wood

A303(T)

Upper Cranbourne Farm

Hunton Down Farm

F G H 131 J K

I
2
3
4
160
5
6
7
8

F G H 184 J K

F G H 133 J K

I

A50

2

3

West Farm

4 P...am

162

5

College Wood

Popham Court Farm

6

Waltham Trinleys

A33

M3

Bradley Farm

Rownest Wood

Woodmanc...

7

Embley Wood

8

Lone Farm

Stevenron Warren Farm

F G H 186 J K

162

PH

Popham Lane

A30

M3

134

D

E

1

A30

Dummer Down Farm

Dummer Down

2

Junction 8

3

4

Popham
Court Farm

Popham

161

The Holt

5

College
Wood

6

†

7

Woodmancott

WEAVERS WAY

8

Lone Farm

A

B

187

C

D

E

1 grid square represents 500 metres

RG25

Goble
Hole

F G H **135** J K

I

2

Nutley

3

4

164

5 ord

Fawkners

B3046

6

Preston House

7

PO Garden
Ct

Preston
Candover
Primary School

Istenbury
Drive

Preston
Candover

8

F G H **188** J K

Warrener's Walk

Dummer Grange

Dummer Grange Farm

Flockmoor
Cottage

Farm

Nutley
Wood

F G H `139` J K

Humbly Grove Copse

Humbly Grove

Blounce

Little Wood

New Farm

`I`

B 3349

`2`

High Wood

Great Parks

Powntley Copse

`3`

Weston Common

B3349

`4`

Shalden Green

Avenue Rd

`168` Gol Pot

`5`

Shalden Park Farm

Old Odiham Road

B3349

`6`

Shalden Park Wood

`7` Golf Club

Stancombe Lane

Golf Course

New Odiham Road

`8`

Fiddler's Fld

Shalden

Southwood

Road

Greenwood Farm

Old Odiham Road

B3349

F G H **141** J K

I

2

Lower
Froyle

3

4

170

5

6

7

8

Froyle Lane

Sutton
Common

Higham Copse

Crest
Hill Farm

Well Lane

Park Lane

Bamber Lane

Hawkins
Wood

Old Lane

Upper
Froyle

Lord Mayor
Treloar College
Lower School

A31

River Wey

PH

combe

Bonham's
Farm

Mill
Court

Cuckoo's
Corner

A31

F G H **194** J K

urne

London Road

River Wey

Styne Farm

Hawbridge Farm

Lane

We

A

B

142

C

D

E

A4
1 Barnfield Cl

Isnage Farm

1
C
Hill

Well Lane

2

Lower
Froyle

Hussey's Lane

3

Husseys Farm

Jenkyn Place

Pax Hill

Bentley

Oakw

Park Lane

4

Bentley
Lane

Bembel
Lane

169

Pax
Hill

A31

5

Highway Home

Be
Gree

Gid

Lane

Isington Lane

Froyle
Mill

6
Lord Mayor
Treloar College
Lower School

A31

River Wey

Isington Road

7

PH

Isington

LC

8

Isington
Road

A

B

195

C

D

E

Broadview

Binstead

The
Street

Court

Binsted C of E
Primary School

ts Cle

I grid square represents 500 metres

A B 157 C D E

Roberts Road

River Dever

Barton Stacey
C of E
Primary School

Tidbury Tomb

1

West Road

East Rd.

Pheasant Cl.

Roman Way

PO

Pentons

Bury's Elm

King's

Gravel Lane

Bullington Lane

Lower
Bullington

comm.

2

Ashfields

Extendsfelds

Barton Stacey

Hill Bam

Barn

Hill

3

4

181

Barton Drove

Cocum Farm

Servic

5

Moody's Down Farm

6

A30

WINCHESTER BY-PASS

A30

7

A272

8

Sutton Down Farm

A B 208 C D E

F4
1 Pigeonhouse Fld
Cross Inn

Upper
Bullington

F G H 158 J K

I

1

2

Hunton
Grange Farm

3

Hunton Down Lane

Cranbourne
Grange

Egypt

Wonston Grange

Hunton Lane

4

Hunton Lane

184

Hunton

Gratton Surgery

Sutton Scotney

River Dever

Stoke
Charity

5

Winchester Road

Oxford Road

Wonston

6

Wonston Lane

East Stoke Road

7

Wonston Manor Farm

8

F G H 209 J K

West Stoke Farm

Wonston Lane

184

A   B   **159**   C   D   E

Hunton
Down Farm

1

Hunton
Grange Farm

2

3

Hunton Down Lane

Norsebury
House

Hunton Lane

4

Hunton

183

Weston
Colley

5   Stoke
Charity

Weston Down Road

River Dever

River Dever

6

Borough F

7

8

Bazle
Copse

A   B   **210**   C   D   E

A B 161 C D E

1

Parkhill Farm

2

Whiteway Farm

Stratton House

West Stratton

3

Church Bank Road

4

PH

East Stratton

Baring Close

185

5

New Farm

6

Burcot Farm

Dodsley Wood

7

Stratton Lane

8

Micheldever Wood

Northington Down Farm

A B 212 C D E

I grid square represents 500 metres

Bradley

F G H **164** J K

I

Preston
Down

2

Lower
Wield

3

Three Castles Path

4

190

5

Three Castles Path

Upper Wield

Home Close

6

Pound

Wield
Wood

7

Three Castles Path

Barton
Copse

Ferney Lane

Armsworth
Hill Farm

Barton
Industrial
Estate

Newmer Farm

8

Ferney Lane

Ferney Lane

Wield Road

Heath Green Lane

Overgrove Way

Berrywood Lane

F G H **215** J K

Hoggs
Lodge

Heath
Green

F　　G　　H　166　J　　K

I
2
3
4
192
5
6
7
8

Wadgett's Copse

Bentworth
Lodge

Drury Lane
Grebe Cl
Glebe Fields

Summerley
PH

St Marys Primary
School

Church St

Village Street

th

Childer
Hill Farm

Heathcroft Farm

olt
nd

Bentworth
Hall

Thedden
Grange

Wivelrod Road

Wellhouse

Wivelrod

Medstead Road

*Bushy-
Leaze
Wood*

Wivelrod Road

King's Hill

The
Abbey

Cem

Old
Park Farm

Abbey Road

Jenner Green Lane

Boxwood Lane

F　　G　　H　217　J　　K

Hussell La

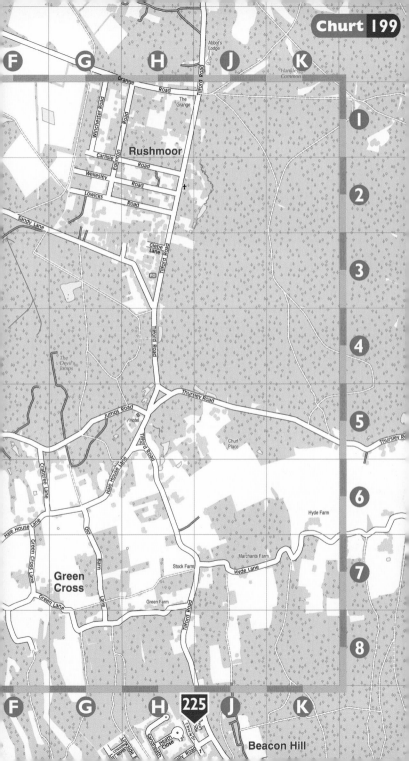

F G H J K

I
2
3
4
5
6
7
8

Abbot's Lodge

Hankley Common

Grange Road

Tilford Road

The Grange

Winchester Road

Eginton Road

Rushmoor

Carlisle Road

Wellesley Road

Lowicks Road

Sandy Lane

Glebe Lane

PO

Tilford Road

The Devil's Jumps

Thursley Road

Jumps Road

Hotel

Tilford Road

Churt Place

Thursley Rd

Hale House Lane

Crabtree Lane

Hyde Farm

Hale House Lane

Old Barn Lane

Green Cross

Stock Farm

Marchants Farm

Hyde Lane

Green Cross Lane

Green Lane

Green Farm

Tilford Road

F G H J K

225

Sandhurst

Heath Close

Churt Rd

Hilly Road

Beacon Hill

F G H **175** J K

I
2
3
4
202
5
6
7
8

ROMSEY

A343

Cottage Road
Sarum Lane
New Rd

Hotel

Jack's
Bush Farm

A343

A343

Drove

Sheep Drove

Wallop Drove

Hollom
Down Farm

A30

Beech Farm

A30

A30

Burretts
Grove

Warren Farm

Broughton
Down

F G H **227** J K

F

G

H 177

J

K

The
...et

143
Danebury Hill

Danebury
Down

I

2

Danebury

3

Houghton
Down

4

204

Chattis
Hill Hō

5

A30   A30

Houghton
Down Farm

Darfield Farm

6

Broughton Road

S020

7

8

F

G

H 229

J

K

Eveley Farm

A B **180** C D E

1

2

New Farm

3

A30

A30

4

A30

205

Sandydown Farm

Heath House

Dumper's Oak

5

6

Busby Copse

B3049

B3049

7

Whitehall Road

8

Winter Down Wood

A B **232** C D E

I grid square represents 500 metres

208

Hill Farm

A272

A

B

182

C

Sutton Down

D

E

1

2

Crawley Down

3

Larkwhistle

4

Warren Woods

207

5

New Barn

6

We Do

7

Beeches Farm

8

Littleton House

Long Park

A

B

234

C

D

E

1 grid square represents 500 metres

F G H 185 J K

I

2

3

4

212

5

6

7

8

Newdown Farm

BASINGSTOKE ROAD

Shroner Wood

Chillandham Lane

Chilandham Lane

Oxdrove Way

Itchen Wood

Michelden Wood

M3

er Hill Farm

M3

Bridgetts Lane

Bridgets Farm

Oxdrove Way

Lone Farm

F G H 237 J K

Couch Green

Old Station Road

School La

Ltl Hayes Lane

Micheldever
Wood

A   B   186   C   D   E

Northington
Down Farm

I

2

Newhouse Farm

3

4

211

5

Oxdrove Way

6

Oxdrove Way

7   arm

Itchen
Down Farm

Itchen
Stoke
Down

Northington Road

Three Castles Path

8

A   B   238   C   D   E

Old Station

Rectory Lane

Baring
Cl

1 grid square represents 500 metres

Totford

F G H **187** J K

Northington

Swarraton

B3046

Swarraton Farm

I

2

3

Abbotstone Down

Ah

nge Park

Waffarer's Walk

4

214

5 Farm

6

Abbotstone

Old Alr ord **7**

Green
Ch

Kiln La

Fobdown Farm

The
rook

8

B3046

Oxdrove Way

Alre

SOU

F G H **239** J K

Wayfarer's Walk

Pinglestone Farm

THE SOKE

Old
Alre
Pon

214

A
B
188
C
D
E

1

Three Castles Path

Godsfield
Copse

Three Castles Path

Godsfield
Farm

2

Spiers Lane

Abbotstone
Woods

3

Abbotstone
Down

Lower
Lanham

4

Warblers's Walk

213

Nettlebed
Farm

5

Coombe Farm

Colden Lane

6

Oxdrove Way

Southdowns

7

d Alresford

Southdowns

Kiln Lane

Colden Lane

Green
Cl

The
Brook

8

B3046

Alresford House

A
SOKE
B
240
C
D
E

Pinglestone Farm

Old

S024

1 grid square represents 500 metres

G6
1 Chalk Cl
2 Thorn Crs
3 Thorn Dr

H4
1 Chawton End Cl

F   G   H   **191**   J   K

I

H5
1 Fairlight Gdns
2 Hazel Rd

2

3

4

218

5

6

7

8

Hussell Lane

Chawton
Park
Wood

Roe
Downs
Farm

Red   Hill
The Crs
Beechlands

Boyneswood Cl

Boyneswood   Road

Boyneswood   Lane

Watercress Line

A31

The Shrave

Brickiln   Lane

WINCHESTER   ROAD

Mansfield
Business
Park

Station   Approach

Staddon
Rise

Fairfield Cln

Boundaries
Surgery

Telegraph   Lane

n Farm
Industrial
Est

Winton

St Thorn   Lane

Blackberry   Lane

Abbotsford
Farm Business
Centre

Weathermore   Lane

Telegraph   Lane

A31
Ecester

**Four
Marks**

Weathermore   Lane

Willis Lane

Headmore
Lane

Headmore Farm

Uplands Lane

Cem

Brislandd

Lymington   Lane

Bottom

Afton Lane

Hawthorn   Lane

Cradwell   Lane

Kitfield Farm

Hawthorn Road

Hawthorn

F   G   H   **243**   J   K

Kitwood   Lane

Kitwood

A   B   192   C   D   E

Old
Park Farm

Winchester

Ja
Ho

Chawton Park Road

Chawtown
Primary School

1

2

Brick ln Lane

A31

Southfield Farm

3

The Shrave

GU34

4

Woodside Lane
Woodside
Farms

Woodside Lane

217

5

Woodside Lane

A32

Lower
Farring

6

Pies Farm

Brightstone Lane

Brightstone Lane

Aviward's Dr

Farringdon
Industrial Centre

Farringdon
Industrial
Est

Ivy Farm

Annetts Farm

7

Kitcombe
Lane

Kitcombe Lane

Headmore Lane

Kitcombe House

8

Headmore Farm

Common
Barn Farm

Mary Lane

Mary Lane

rthorn Lane

Newton
Common

A   B   244   C   Pelham
Place   D   E

A32

GREEN STREET

FORGE RD B3004

Oaklands Farm

Lode Farm

Oxney Farm

Kingsley Stream

F **G** **H** **195** **J** **K**

Binswood

Rookery Farm

Gibbs Lane

Shortheath Common

Shortheath

Old Station Way

Bolley Av

Cem

Bordon Trading Est

Oakhanger Road

Binswood View Business Cen

Oakhanger

Honey Lane

Hogmoor Road

Hogmoor Inclosure

222

Slab

The Warren

Moor Cl

Spruce Avenue

Cypress Rd

Mornington Rd

Juniper Cl

Selborne Way

Warren Close

Mornington Rd

Chapel Farm

The Spur

Granary St

Sandy Rd

Terrace

Oak Lane

Firgrove Road

Blackmoor Golf Club

St Groves

The Dray

Heath

Drift Road

Plantation Way

Eveley Cl

Honey Lane

Albury Farm

St Matthews C of E Primary School

F **G** **H** **247** **J** Blackmoor **K**

222

FORD

196

221

248

C5
1 Lavender Gdns
2 Manica Cl
3 Tilbury's Cl
4 Woodside Crs

C6
1 Connaught Cl
2 Dene Cl
3 Melrose Cl
4 Nutley Cl

C7
1 Bedford Cl
2 Nthumberld Rd
3 Richmond Cl

D4
1 Beavers Ms

D5
1 Blackthorne Cl
2 Ferncote Rd
3 Norman Cl
4 Primula Rd

D6
1 Amber Cl
2 Chestnut Ct
3 Ducklands
4 Foxglove Dr
5 Hendon Rd
6 Hibiscus Gv
7 Jasmine Wy
8 Kingfisher Cl
9 Magpie Cl
10 Neptune Rd
11 Nightingale Rd

C3
1 Bassenthwte Gdn
2 Buttermere Cl
3 Derwent Cl
4 Grasmere Cl
5 Thirlmere Cl

B7
1 Mayflower Rd
2 Petersfield Rd

A7
1 Gorsedown Cl

E3
1 Cricket Lea
2 Five Acres Cl

E4
1 Greenacres

E5
1 Britannia Cl
2 Mercury Cl

A   B   C   D   E

1   2   3   4   5   6   7   8

Bordon

Whitehill

1 grid square represents 500 metres

224

198

223

250

198

A B C D E

B4
1 Gorselands Cl
2 Telconia Cl
3 Witherslack Cl

B3
1 Penryn Dr

A2
1 Eddeys Cl
2 Embleton Rd

Churt Road

Barford

Hearn

Hearn Rd Lane

Langton Drive

The Mount

Mow Hill

Arford Cott

Arford Common

eech

Hill

Glaysher's Cl

Hillside Cl

Alger Road

Birch Rd

Marle Way

Larch Rd

Pine Vw

Ling Crs

Eddeys La

Windmill Dr

B3002

Headley Hill Road

BEECH HILL B3002

Southview Road

Wilsons Rd

PO

Fairview

Honeysuckle La

Kenley Road

Linden Road

Furze Vale Rd

Headley Down

Stonehill Pk

Furze Hill

Pond Road

GRAYSHOTT

ROAD

Holly Rd

Alma Rd

West Vw Rd

Carlton Road

Seymour Road

Seymour Cl

Birkenholme Cl

Rixonside

B3002

Hammer Lane

Whit

Grayshott Hall

Ludshott Common

Fairway

Fox Way

B3002

Gentles Lane

Gentle's Copse

Gentles Lane

Woolmer Farm

Summerden

We

Ludshott Manor

Oaklea Farm

Downlands

urgh Road

Woolmer

A B C D E

Rectory Lane

Limes Close

VALE

Vale

stside

chestside

s La

Lar La

I grid square represents 500 metres

North Houghton

204

Marsh Court

Houghton Lodge

Church Lane

River Test

Stevens Drove

Houghton

Faithfulls Drove

Clarendon Way

Hoopers Farm

Test Way

229

Bossington

Horsebridge Road

Horsebridge Road

Ki
Somb

Hayes Close

River Test

Horsebridge

Test Way

Horsebridge Road

ROMSEY

ROAD

ROMSEY ROAD

Compton Park

258

Compton Manor

Humbers Wood

Compton

F5
1 Nutchers Dro

North
Park Farm

F

G

H

205

J

K

Down
Copse

North
Park
Wood

1

Little
Somborne House

2

Little
Somborne

3

Hill

New
Lease Farm

4

Clark Vale
Farm

232

New Lane

Road

5

Winchester

Ashley

Road

6

Eldon
Close

7

Furzedown

Clarendon Way

Road

Ashley
Down

Hooplands

Clarendon Way

8

Furzedown
Road

F

G

H

259

J

K

Furzedown

Luke Copse

232

A   B **206** C   D   E

1

Winter
Down
Copse

Little
Somborne House

2   †

Chalk Hill

3

Rookley
Manor

Court Lane

Up Somborne

4   Chalk Vale

Chalk Vale
Farm

231

5

Ashley

6   †

Ashley
Wood

Great Up
Somborne Wood

7

8   Ashley
Down

Forest of Bere Farm

Farley
Mount

A   B **260** C   D   E

Clarendon

Clarendon Way

I grid square represents 500 metres

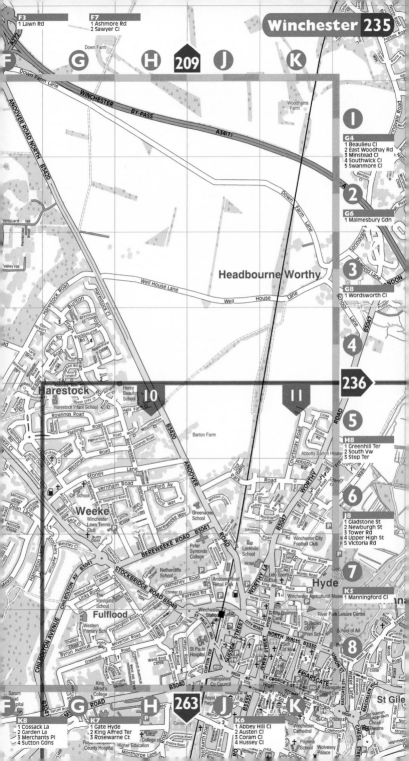

F G H 211 J K

Couch
Green

Old Station
Road

School La

Ltl Hayes
Lane

Itchen
Abbas CP
School

I

B3047

STATION

Station
Cl

HILL

Three Castles Path

Martyr
Worthy

Church Lane

Chilland Lane

Chilland

Shelley
Cl

King's Way

2

Itchen
Abbas

River Itchen

3

Avington
Park

Avington

PH

Easton

4

238

5

Mud Farm

6

Chapel Lane

7

air Lane

Larkwhistle Farm

Pits Farm

8

's

F B3404 G H 265 J A31 K

Cemetery

A31

242

216

Ropley Sol

North Street

Ropley Dean

Dean Surgery
Hook

241

Ropley

Gilbert Street

Rowden Cott

Ropley C of E
Primary School

Lyewood Ho

Harcombe

Soames Farm

Bramdean
Common

270

West Tisted

I grid square represents 500 metres

F G H **217** J K

I

Hawthorn

Headmore Farm

Mar

Cradwell
Lane

Alton Lane

Kitfield Farm

Hawthorn

Hawthorn Lane

Bottom

Lane

Kitwood

Kitwood Lane

2

welling Hill

Hawthorn Road

Redbridge Lane

Kitwood Road

Dogford
Wood

3

Lyeway Lane

Lyeway Rd

Lyeway Farm

Winchester
Wood

Rod

4

Plain Farm

Green
Lane

Charlwood Lane

244

Plaindell

5

Charlwood

Petersfield Road

6

Monkwood

Petersfield Road

Hill Farm Road

ame's Lane

Lane

Hill Farm Road

7

d Farm

West
Tisted
Common

Woodside Farm

Brewers

8

Brick
Kiln Farm

Brick Kiln

Lane End

Brewers Lane

F G H **271** J K

F
G
H
219
J
K

Selbor

Inadown Farm

Newton Lane

I

Shotters Lane

Shotters Farm

2

Newton Valence Place

Selborne Hanger

Se Co

Longhope

Lowe Hill F

Newton Valence

Hullam Lane

3

Heards Farm

Charity Farm

4

246

Goleigh Wood

5

Goleigh Farm

6

Vann Farm

Button's Lane

Keyham Farm

Slade Farm

7

Church Farm

8

Manor House

F
G
H
273
J
K

246

Gracious Street

Selborne Primary School

Pendulum Gallery

A

Selborne

B

220

C

D

E

New Barn Farm

Honey Lane

1

Selborne Hanger

Selborne Common

Hangers Way

2

Ketchers Fld

Sotherington Lane

Burhunt Farm

3

Lower Noar Hill Farm

Hangers Way

4

Charity Farm

245

Mill Lane

5

Hangers Way

Empshott Green

Empshott

Church

Boleigh Farm

6

Keyriam Farm

Vann Farm

Hangers Way

Mill Lane

Lythanger

7

Hawkley Hurst

8

Mill Lane

Earl's Lane

Upland

Lowergreen Farm

Hawkley

A

Hangers Way

B

274

C

Hawkley Road

D

E

Scotland Farm

PH

POcocks Lane

1 grid square represents 500 metres

J2
1 Sunvale Cl

J3
1 Hammerwd Cps
2 Puttock Cl

F

G

H

225

J

K

Bramshot Common

PORTSMOUTH ROAD

Hammer Lane

Woolmer Hill

Woolmer Hill School

Critchmere Hill

Critchmere

Holy Cross Hosp

I

K2
1 Lucas Fld
2 Mallard Cl
3 Mill Cl
4 Pitfold Cl

Shot

B2131

2

HINDHEAD

Vicarage Lane Clinic

Lower Hanger

Woolmer Hill Rd

Hatchetts Drive

Cemetery

Fir Tree Avenue

Sunvale Av

Oak Tree Lane

Border Rd

Pitfold Av

LIPHOOK RD

The Millstream

Camelsdale County First School

3

Hammer Lane

Hammer Bottom

Copse Road

Heath Rd

Moor Rd

Hammer Lane

LINCHMERE ROAD

B2131

B2131

CAMELSDALE RD

Hammer

Cemetery

Gillham's Lane

ROAD

LIPHOOK

Linchmere Road

Linchmere Common

Penwith Drive

Marley Lane

4

252

Marley Common

Danley Lane

Sussex Border Path

Sussex Border Path

Marley House

5

Linchmere

Cognor Wood

6

Kings

7

Marle

Stanley Farm

Greenhill Wood

8

F

G

H

J

K

Oakreeds Wood

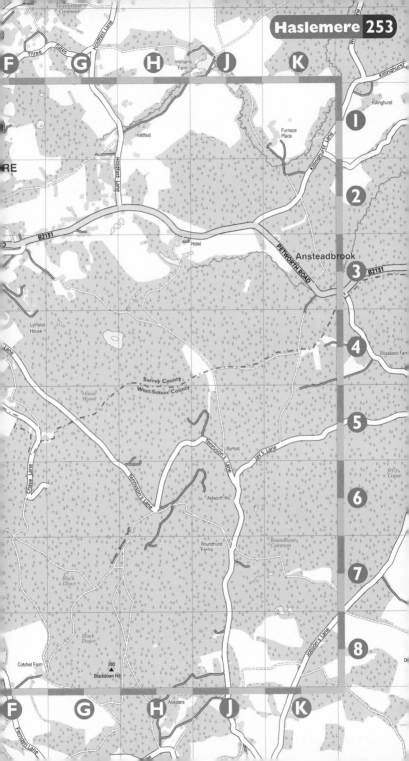

F G H J K

Graywood Common

Three Gates

Holdfast Lane

Imbhams Farm

I

Killinghurst

Killinghurst

Killinghurst Lane

Holdfast

Furnace Place

2

Holdfast Lane

B2131

Hotel

PETWORTH ROAD

Ansteadbrook

3 B2131

Lythehill House

4

Boxalland Farm

Lane

Surrey County
West Sussex County

Home Wood

5

Tennyson's Lane

Barfold

Jay's Lane

Jay's Copse

Chase Lane

6

Aldworth Ho

Tennyson's Lane

Sussex Border Path

Roundhurst Farms

Roundhurst Common

7

Black Down

Jobson's Lane

Black Down

8

Cotchet Farm

280
Blackdown Hill

Di

F G H J K

Abesters

Fernden Lane

Standing Hill
Home Farm
West Tytherley Primary School
West Tytherley
Stride's Farm

227

The Coach Road
The Coach Road

The Green

Dean Lane
Red Lane
Dean Road
Burk's Hole
Pug's Hole
Bills Drove

Tytherley Common
Frenchmoor

Drove Farm Ho

Pug's Hole Farm

Frenchmoor Lane

Holbury Farm
Holbury
256
Holbury Lane

Frenchmoor La
Park Farm

East

LC
East Dean
Cliphe Mdw

Deanhill Barn

Gatmore Copse
Hampshire C
Cooks Lane

283

256

Stony Batter

228

Manor Farm

The Coach Road

Manor Rd

East Tytherley

Cedars Vw

Lockerley Hall

Lain Copse

255

Holbury

Holbury La

Holbury Lane

Holbury Mill

Lockerley Water Farm

River Dunn

River Dun

Dean Road

East

LC

Lockerley

Lockerley C of E Primary School

Lockerley Rd

Pendle

Cooks Lane

Butt's Green

Critchell's Green

Cooks Lane

Mount Lane

284

1 Butlers Cl

D7

1 grid square represents 500 metres

Hoplands

Clarendon

Ashley
Down

I

Luke Copse

Furzedown

2

Parnholt
Wood

3

Furzec
Road

Bailey's
Down

4

Eldon Ho

Fishponds Fm

260

5

Farley Ho

Tubbs
Copse

Eldon Road

Parnell Lane

6

Hall Place

Furzedown Road

7

Monarch's Way

Kings Somborne Road

Pitt Fm

Farley Lane

Eldon Road

Haydon Road

Braishfield Road

8

Monarch's Way

Fern Hill Lane

Paynes
Hay

Paynes Hay
Farm

Church Lane

Sharpes Fm

Lower St

Rudd Lane

Dummers Rd

Monarch's Way

A   B   232   C   D   E

Ashley Down

Forest of Bere Farm

Farley Mount

1

Luke Copse

Clarendon Way

2

Parnholt Wood

Mount Down

3

Farley Down

Bailey's Down

4

Farley Fm

Berrydown Farm

259

+

5

Farley Ho

Dores Lane

Oakfield

Dores Lane

6

Cudge Copse

7

Upper Slackstead

Dores Lane

8

Hill Lane

A   Lower Sla B tea 288 C   D   E

Dores Lane

Carroll Road

Woolley Green Fm

1 grid square represents 500 metres

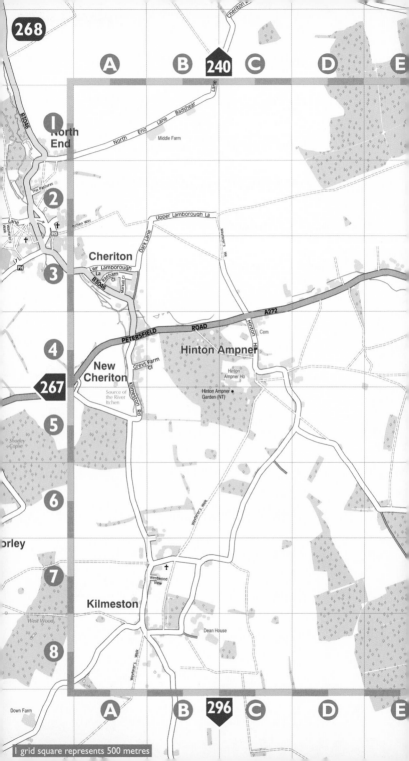

F
G
H
241
J
K

I

2

Bramdean Common

Old Park Wood

Old Park Road

Wood Lane

Marriners Farm

Wood Farm

Wolfhanger Farm

3

Bramdean

The Spinney

Wood Lane

Woodlane Close

A272

PH

Woodcote Manor House

Tithelands Lane

Slys Farm

4

270
Woodlands Farm

5

Joan's Acre

The Dean

A272

6

Brockwood Park

Brockwood Bottom

Shutt's Copse

7

8

F
G
H
297
Bere Farm
J
K

Markdell Farm

270

A   B   **242**   C   D   E

I

Bramdean
Common

2

Wolfhanger Farm

3

Slys Farm

4

269

Purser's

Hinton
Woodlands Farm

5

The
Dean

6

A272

Kitt's Lane

**West Meon
Woodlands**

Woodlands Farm

7

Shutt's
Copse

West
Meon Hut

A272

8

Highfield

Mardell Farm

A   B   **298**   C   D   E

Conway Road

West Tisted

Green La

PO

Punsholt Lane

Punsholt Farm

Punsholt Lane

A32

Three Horse
Shoes Farm

Three Horse Shoes Lane

Vinnells Lane

Hayling
Wood

I grid square represents 500 metres

Woodside Farm

F G H **243** J K
Lane End

Brick
Kiln Farm

Brick Kiln Lane

Brewers Lane

I

Basing
Park

A32

2

Basing
Home Farm

The
Jumps

3

Sates Lane

Ashen
Wood House

Basing Dean

4

Fawley Farm

Fawley Lane

Hemplund Lane

re Hill

272

Bailey Green

Filmorehill Lane

Farnfield Farm

Merepond Lane

Church Lane

PO

5

Stocks Lane

Privett

✝

6

Stock Farm

Stocks Lane

7

A272

8

F G H **299** J K

Old
Down Farm

Woodside Farm

A   B   244   C   D   E

Coleman
Common

Hermitage

1

Basing
Park

Clavpitt Lane

2

3

Basing Dean

Coles

Alexander's Farm

Basing Dean

4

271

Farnfield Farm

Mershond Lane

5

Hurst Farm

Hurst

Lane

Woolfield Lane

King's

Lane

6

Bower Farm

7

Bydean Farm

High Cross Lane

High Cross Lane

8

Broad   Way

Froxfield
Green

Staple   Ash   Lane

A   B   300   C   D   E

I grid square represents 500 metres

F G H 245 J K

Manor House

I

2

Five Ash Farm

Warren Farm

The Warren

Oakshott Farm

Warren Lane

3

Barnet Side

Oaksho

Warren Corner

Hill Farm

4

274

Green Lane

Lane

5

Blackmoor Lane

Lane

Honeycritch

Lane

Old Litten Lane

rnhouse Lane

vyhouse Farm

Bensgreen Farm

PH

Binsgreen Lane

Cockshott Lane

6

The Slade

High Cross Lane

Week Green Farm

Hangers Way

xfield wed Controlled ant School

Deans

Deans

High Cross

Wyke Green Farm

7

Scotwood Lane

Broadhanger

King Lane

Stoner Hill

8

Island

Broad Way

Ridge Top Lane

Church Common

F G r's Farm H 301 J K

Stonerwood Park

Ridge Top Lane

Lane

Croucheston Drove

High Road

Flamston

Butt Lane

Harvest La

The Croft

The Styles

Pitts La

Lane Alley

Netton St

Lane

chesston

Chapel La

Bridge Drove

The Cross

Bishopstone

F G H J K

1

2

3

Faulston Down

4

280

Faulstone Down Farm

5

A354

Croucheston Down Farm

6

T C

Hampshire County

Wiltshire County

7

Swayne's Firs

A354

Grimsdyke Granaries

8

F G H 305 J K

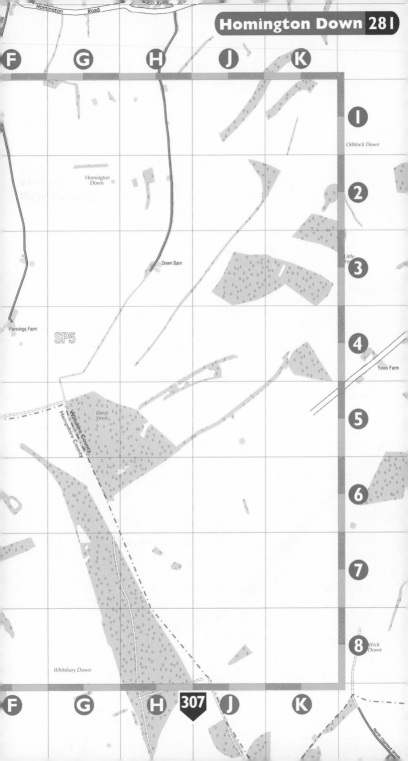

254

A B C D E

1

2

Alderstone Farm

3

C4
y 1 The Triangle

Mean Wood

Miles's Lane

Ashmore Lane

Miles's Lane

4

BRICKWORTH

ROAD

A27 THE STREET

Pill Hill

Ashmore Ho

Nunns Park

Whiteparish

PO

Whiteparish Surgery

Ashmore Ct

Ashmore Green

Dean Lane

Highlands Way

A27 ROMSEY ROAD

Meadow Ct

5

Newton Close

Doves Lane

Newton Lane

Clay Street

Croft Hts

Whiteparish All Saints C of E Primary School

The Brambles

Common Rd

Cowesfield G

6

Newton

A36(T)

Hool Lane

Lowdens Copse

Common Fm

7

Glazier Copse

Whiteparish Common

Common Road

Parkwater Road

8

Earldoms Lodge

Bagfield Copse

A B C D E

312

Scotland Lane

Stock Lane

1 grid square represents 500 metres

F G H **257** J K

I
2
3
4
286
5
6
7
8

F G H **315** J K

River Dun
River Dun
Mill Rise
Lockerley Road
DUNE
LANE
Monarch's Way
Kimbridge Lane
Kimbridge Lane
LC
River Test
B3084
Hyde Fm
Saunders Lane
Awbridge Ho
Lockerley Road
Kents Oak
Test Way
Awbridge County School
Danes Road
Awbridge
Cooks
Lane
STANBRIDGE
Upper Ratley
Church
Lane
Coombe Lane
Lower Ratley
Stanbridge Earls School
Awbridge Danes
Dunwood Manor Golf Club
Dunwood Manor
Danes Road
Roke Manor Fm
Old Salisbury Lane
Test Way
Shootash
Stanbridge Ranvilles Fm
Roke Manor
Squabb Wood
Tanners Lane
A27
Embley Lane
Spursholt Ho

F G H **259** J K

Low

1
F7
1 Carisbrooke Ct
2 Homefield
3 Smith's Fld
4 Waterside Rd

Puckhall

2
F8
1 Greenwood Cl
2 Latham Rd
3 Mercer Wy
4 Nelson Cl

3
G6
1 Cavendish Cl

4

288

5
G7
1 Clarendon Cl
2 Nogarth Cl
3 Savernake Cl
4 Sutherland Cl
5 Tavistock Cl
6 Waverley Cl

6
G8
1 Barton Cl
2 Brickwoods
3 Harefield Ct
4 Nerquis Cl
5 St Blaize Rd
6 Strongs Cl
7 Windfield Dr

7
H6
1 Anderson Cl
2 Ganger Rd
3 The Green
4 Norris Cl
5 Woodley Wy

Cran

8
H7
1 Abbotswood Cl
2 Beverley Gdns
3 Bramble Dr
4 Coltsfoot Wk
5 Primrose Wy
6 South Cl
7 Westering
8 Winterbourne Rd

Braishfield

Sharpes La

Rudd Lane

Lower St

Paynes Hay Farm

Paynes Hay

Braishfield Road

Church Lane

Newport Lane

Common Hill Road

Monarch's Way

Dummers Rd

Fern

Hill Vw Rd

Braishfield CP School

Kiln Lane

Megana Wy

Fairbornes Fm

Abbotswood Fm

Jermyns Ho

Jermyns Lane

Sandy Lane

Braishfield Road

Ibins siness Park

Abbotswood

Cemetery

Ganger Fm

A3090

THE STRAIGHT MILE

MILE

Woodley Close

Woodley Lane

Woodley Lane

Horseshoe Dr

Hunters

School Road

Peel Cl

Woodley

Crampmoor Lane

Green Lane

LC

ham

Brook Way

Richmond Lane

Kinver Cl

Kinver Dr

Dansie Cl

Carisbrooke Cl

Carisbrooke Dr

Winterbourne

Fairview Dr

Fairview

Juniors & Infant School

Durban Cl

Cupernham Close

Cupernham Lane

WINCHESTER RD

Winchester Rd

Romsey County Junior School

htingale

WINCHESTER HILL

The Crs

Viney Wy

Ashley Mdw

Selsdon Av

Romsey Hospital

A3090

Stroud School

Highwood

Crampmoor

La

LC

Eight Acres

Seward Ri

Jenner Wy

Kennett

Halterworth Lane

Hestia

Botley Road

Cemetery

317

F G H J K

1 St Swithun's Cl
2 Winchester Rd

Halterworth CP School

rth

H8
1 Seward Ri
2 Westering

Whitenap

Warren Fm

A B 260 C D E

I

Lower Slackstead

Dover Lane
Clayon Road

Woolley
Green Fm

Monarch's Way

Monarch's Way

Ampfield
Wood

2

Pucknall

Clayon Road

3

4

Jermyns Ho

Knapp Lane

Ampfield
Primary
School

Kn

A3090

Ampfield

A3090

Green Pond
Lane

5

South
Holmes
Copse

A3090

THE STRAIGHT MILE

6

Gosport

Pound Lane

7

crampmoor

LC

Crampmoor

8

Green Lane

Stroud
School

Pound Lane

A B 318 C D Bucket Cor

Baddesley
Common

Warren Fm

F G H **261** J K

I

Hursley

Home Farm

Hursley Park

Poot Lane

Collins Lane

Monarch's Way

Cemetery

Shawlands Far

Bunstead **2**

I6
1 Clevelands Cl
2 Rothville Pl
3 Tithewood Cl

South End Close

Poles Lane

B3043

Keble Memorial Primary School

Monarch's Way

3

J7
1 Albury Pl
2 Apsley Pl
3 Chillington Gdns
4 Lauriston Dr
5 Stratfield Dr
6 The Tanyards
7 Vanburgh Wy

4

Ladwell

Field House

Batsake Lane

HURSLEY ROAD

290

5

Home Farm

I8
1 Balmoral Cl
2 Barford Cl
3 Drummond Wy
4 Polesden Cl

Ratlake

Hook Road

Hawstead Farm

Monks Brook

B3043

...adgate

Woodlea Way

Hook Road

Hook Crescent

Hook Water Road

Hocombe Wood Road

HURSLEY ROAD

Hocombe Road

Hocombe Road

Hocombe

Charnwood Cl

Maytree Rd

Ashdown

Roads

6 Hiltingbur

K6
1 Charnwood Gdns

Beechwood Close

Beechwood Crescent

Charnwood Cl

Heathfield Road

Sycamore Close

Queen's Road

Randall

Woodlands

Fishers Copse

Birchglade

Sandown

Avenue

Hiltingbury Road

Sycamore Avenue

PO

7

North

...Road

Gor... Road

Pine Road

Hiltingbury County Junior & Infant School

Beech Road

Chand Ford

Flexford

Millers Dale Surgery

Leigh House

Leigh House Hospital

Bushes Lane

Cuckoo ...

Carne

Paulton

Linden Grove

Road

Sherborne House School

Lakewood Road

Merdon

Adamscroft Close

Millers...

B3043

Common

Merdon...Sur

Flexford Road

Menarch's Way

Knightwood Primary School

Bowland Rise

319 J K

Cemetery

Ike...

Common

Road

Heathlands Road

Park Road

Valley Road

Kingsway

Woodhill Preparatory School

Brownhill Road

Merdon Junior Sch

Skid Wood Road

Knightwood Farm

HURSLEY R...

S053

Marchester

Carlyn Drive

Purkess Close

Paetlands

Brue...

Merdichen Drive

The Bro...

F G H J K

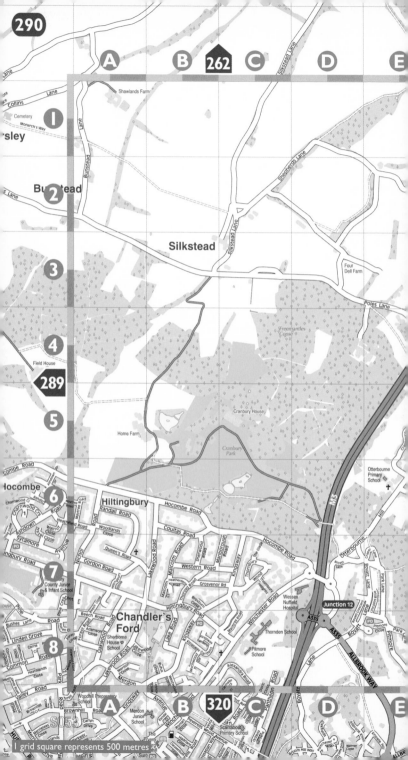

Otterbourne 291

Grid references and labels

- **F** **G** **H** **263** **J** **K**
- **F** **G** **H** **321** **J** **K**

Places
- Compton
- Compton All Saints C of E Primary School
- Shawford
- Shawford House
- Shawford Station
- South Down
- Richmond Park
- Twyford
- Twyford Lodge
- Twyford School
- Twyford C of E Primary School
- Twyford Moors
- Twyford Surgery
- Northfields
- Brambridge
- Brambridge House
- Highbridge
- Colden Common
- Colden Common Primary School
- St Vigor
- Nob's Crook

Numbered locations
- **I** Northfields
- **2**
- **F5** 1 Meadowcroft Cl
- **3**
- **K1** 1 Franklin Rd 2 Penton Rd
- **4**
- **292**
- **5**
- **K2** 1 St Mary's Ter
- **6**
- **7** Colden Common
- **8**

Roads (selection)
- M3
- B3335
- B3354
- Winchester Road
- Hurdle Way
- Otterbourne Road
- Southdown Road
- Fairfield Road
- Cross Way
- Grove Road
- Waterworks Road
- Shepherds Lane
- Kiln Lane
- Church Lane
- Highbridge Road
- Main Road
- Bridge Road
- Searles Hill
- Thorn Town
- Bourne Lane
- Hazeley Road
- Love Lane
- Park Lane
- High St
- Queen Street
- Berry Lane
- Old Rectory Lane
- Hare Lane
- Woodland Drove
- New Road
- Boyes Lane
- Lower Moors Road
- Piping Road
- Valley Close
- Nob's Crook
- The Itchen Navigation
- River Itchen

F G H 269 J K

I
2
3
4
298
5
6
7
8

Bere Farm

Marldell Farm

ely Farm

Lippen Cotts

Long Priors

Floud La

Maaons

Chu

West M
Contro
Primary Se

West Meor

Warnford

Lippen Lane

Old Winchester Hill Lane

Monarch's Way

Warnford
Park

Monarch's Way

Old Winchester Hill Lane

Peake New Road

Peake Farm

A32

F G H 327 J K

xton

ns Way

South Downs Way

A
B
280
C
D
E

Little
Toyd Down

Toyd Farm

Tenantry Farm

Paradise

1

Rockbourne
Down

2

3

Duck's
Nest

Knap
Barrow

Grans
Barrow

4

Toyd
Down

Down Farm

305

5

Glebe

Knoll
Down

6

7

North Allenford Farm

Damerham
Knoll

8

Knoll Farm

A
B
336
C
D
E

South
Allenford Farm

Allen River

I grid square represents 500 metres

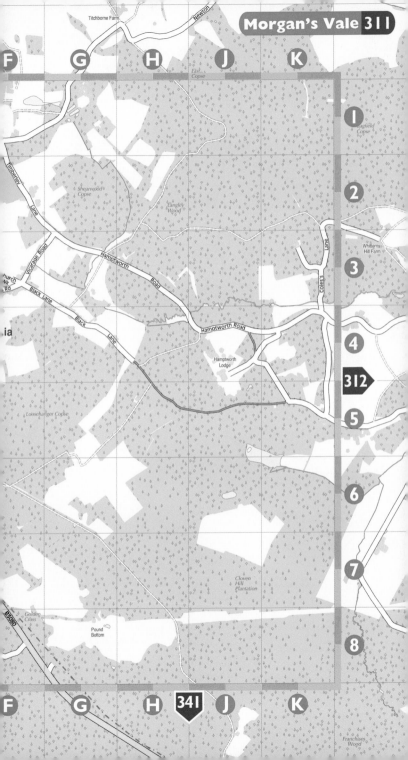

F G H J K

I

Ragfield
Copse

2

*East
Copse*

*Cangley
Wood*

Whitlems
Hill Farm

3

Titchborne Farm

Newton

*Shearwood
Copse*

Timberley
Lane

Vicarage Road

Hamptworth

Road

Church
Nk
Rd

Black Lane

Coles's
Lane

Black

Lane

Hamptworth Road

Hamptworth
Lodge

4

312

5

Looseharger Copse

6

7

*Cloven
Hill
Plantation*

Golden
Cross

B3080

Pound
Bottom

8

F G H **341** J K

*Franchises
Wood*

F G H 283 J K

Wellow Wood Road

Plaitford Green

I

Steplake

Park Water

Compton's Drive

Bowles Farm

English Lane

Dover Lane

Sherfield Lane

2

Spouts Lane

Steplake

Manor Farm

Church Lane

Pound Lane

Pound Hill

Giles Lane

River Blackwater

Sherfield English La

3

Landford Manor

4

Lane

314

Kitchen Close

Bourne Close

The Beeches

Plaitford

Sherfield English Road

PARTRIDGE HILL

A36(T)

SALISBURY

Purlieu Way

New Road

ROAD

5

6

Plaitford Common

West Wellow Common

7

8

Plantation Rd

Canada Common

Barford Farms

F G H 343 J K

316

286

C

D1
1 Abbey Water
2 Corn Market
3 Narrow La
4 Palmerston St
5 Spring Pl

E1
1 Fleming Pl
2 Knatchbull Cl
3 Palmerston St
4 Pembroke Cl

315

346

Moorcourt

1 grid square represents 500 metres

Romsey 317

F1
1 Jacobs Cl
2 Nursery Gdns
3 Oakleigh Gdns
4 Tadburn Cl

F2
1 Petty Cl
2 St Barbe Cl
3 Sydmanton Cl
4 The Tyleshades

G1
1 Eight Acres
2 Halterworth Cl
3 Hereward Cl
4 Nightingale Cl
5 The Vikings

H1
1 Montfort Heights

H2
1 The Thicket

K3
1 Broad La
2 Highlands Cl
3 Overbrook Wy

Halterworth
Whitenap
Ashfield
Toothill
Lee
Upton
Rownhams

318

A **B** **288** **C** **D** **E**

Bucket Corner

1
Warren Fm
A2
1 Stragwyne Cl

Baddesley
Common

Flexford Road

2
LEY ROAD
A3
1 Heatherview Cl
2 Pine Cl

BOTLEY ROAD

S052

Nutburn
Road

Sandy La

Nutburn

3
West Lane
Broad La
A4
1 Heatherbrae Gdn
2 Northerwood Cl
3 Tutland Rd
4 Woodside Rd

Baddesley Park
Industrial Est

Castle Lane

Great Co

4
Cerne Cl
Queens Ride

**North
Baddesley**

County
Infants
School
North Baddesley
Junior School
Norton Welch Close

BOTLEY ROAD

Misslebrook Lane

317
Hoe Fm

Health
Centre

A27

BOTLEY ROAD

5
B3
1 Emer Cl

**Chilworth
Old Village**

Fowler's
Wk

6
Telegraph
C3
1 Sandy La

Tanner's Brook

Parkway

Toothill

7
E6
1 Woodside Crs

Rownhams Lane

Pacroup
Lane

University
Venture
Drive
Chilworth
Drive

Southampton
University

Man

8
Toothill
Rd
Greenhill Lane

Rownhams Service Area

M27

Rownhams Service Area

Chilworth

N

A **B** **348** **C** **D** **E**

Horns Drove
Acorn
Dr
Routy
Way

St

Rownhams

Lord's
Wood

1 grid square represents 500 metres

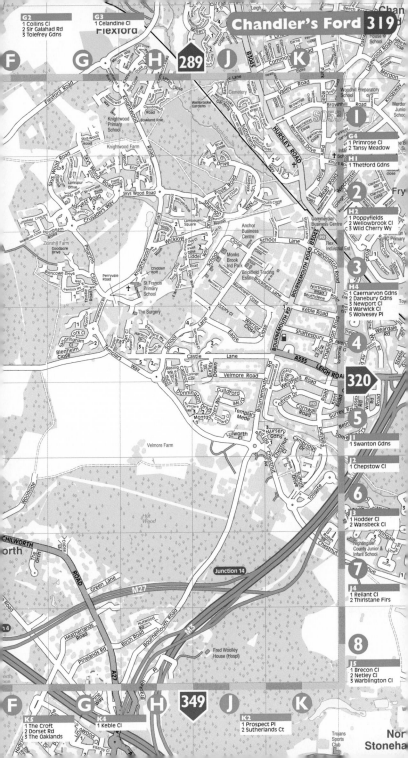

F
Marwell House
G
H 293
J
Woodlock
Down Farm
K

Farm

Rowhay
Wood

Monarch's Way

Roughay Farm

Hatchley Lane

Rowhay
Lane

West
Hall

Widlers La

Upham
School

1

Upham
2
Cem

Church Stree

3

OAD
B2177

Popes   Lane

Upham Farm

Stroudwood Farm

Stroudwood   Lane

PORTSMOUTH ROAD

B5037

LANE

Upham Street

Upham Street

King's Way

4

324
Stakes Farm

5

Stakes Lane

Stakes La

udwood
ry Farm

Lower Upham

PO

B2177

WINCHESTER ROAD

Woolstreet Farm

6

Alma Lane

Crescent

Sciver's Lane

Wintershill
Hall

King's Way

7

Durley   Hall
Lane

Durley
Hall Farm

Wintershill

Winter's Hill

wood Lane

Sciver's Lane

Durley Street

8 **Newt**

Durley Street

THE Drove

King's Way

F
G
H 353
J
Road
K

Manor

Durley Manor Farm

Tangier Farm

324

294

A B C D E

1

Woodlock's
Down Farm

Woodcote

Belmore House

Monarch's Way

Bigpath Farm

Upham

Shoe Lane

Cem

Widleys La

Church street

2

King's La

West
Hall

Upham
School

Upham Street

King's La

3

Peak Lane

Stakes Lane

Monarch's Way

Street End

King's Way

4

323

5

Stakes Farm

Peak Lane

Highfield Farm

B8
1 Cunningham Av
2 Hermitage Cl

Stakes Lane

Cross Lane

Ashton

ROAD

6

Vernon Hill House

Spindlecroft

Beeches

C8
1 Claylands Rd
2 Edington Cl
3 Princes Cl
4 St Swithun Cl

Cross
Lanes Farm

Ashton Lane

Vernon Hill

Vernon Hill

Northbrook

7

Roke Farm

Portsdge Lane

D8
1 Denewulf Cl
2 Middlebrook
3 St Bonnet Dr

The Coach
Station

BISHOP'S WALTHAM

8

Withy Hill

Newtown

Tangier Lane

Gravatom Business
Centre

Merlin

Langton Road

B3035

LOWER LANE

Free Street

The Surg

Meon Valley
Police
Station

A B C D E

354

Bishop's Palace
(remains of)

Bishop's
Lane

COPPICE HILL B2177

B2177

Manor Farm

The Drove

1 grid square represents 500 metres

326

A **B** **296** **C** **D** **E**

Dawlileaze Copse

Winters Down

Sailor's Lane

Be Hill Lane

South Downs Way

Lone Barn Lane

1

Corhampton Forest

The White Way

Corhampto

2

Bottom Copse

B3035

Steynes Farm

Corha

3

CORHAMPTON LANE

B3035 CORHAMPTON LANE

Corhampton Golf Club

4

Golf Club Bungalow

Wayfarer's Walk

Haze

325

5

Sheep Pond Lane

Sheep Pond

Shepherds Down

Hacketts

Sheep Pond

Cem Car Pk

6

Lane

Hacketts Lane

Northend Lane

Car

Waltham Close

Union

Chestnut

A32

7

Park Lane

Doctors Surgery

Droxford

The Dene

Mill

Droxford Primary School

Pack

Wayfarers

HIGH ST

Wayfarer's Walk

Droxford Junior School

8

Swanmore Park House

Mayhill Lane

South Hill Lane

A32

MIDLINGTON ROAD

Upper Swanmore

Green Lane

A **B** **356** ord **C** **D** Midlington Ho **E**

La

Mayhill Farm

Mayhill Lane

Swanmore Road

Midlington Hill

Midlington Hill

Cutts

I grid square represents 500 metres

Peake Farm

A   B   298   C   D   E

South Downs Way

South Downs Way

Whitewool Farm

1

2

South Downs Way

South Downs Way

south

Monarch's Way

Monarch's Way

3

199
Old Winchester Hill

Stock S

Stocks

4

Teglease
Down

327

Little West End
Fm

5

Westend
Down

6

Teglease Fm

Sheardley Lane

Stoke Wood

7

Whiteleaf
Lane

8

Big West
End Fm

Chidd

Stoke Wood

Green Lane

Grenville
Hall

A   B   358   C   D   E

Green Lane

Whiteleaf
Lane

1 grid square represents 500 metres

East Meon

Coombe Road

F
G
H
J
K

Lower
House Farm

South Downs Way

Oxenbo

I

Coombe
Cross

2

South Farm

3

South Downs Way

233
▲
Salt Hill

4

330

Chidden Down

5

South Downs Way

South Downs Way

Way

Old
Hambledonians
Cricket Club

6

Hyden Farm Lane

Hyden
Wood

Coombe
Wood

7

Monarch's Way

8

Hyden Farm Lane

Hyden Farm

F
G
H
J
K

North Fm

Monarch's Way

Farm Lane

A
B
C
D
E

Lower
House Farm

Leythe House

Oxenbourne House

1

Limekiln Lane

2

South Farm

Harvesting Lane

Limekiln Lane

Stonylands Farm

3

Harvesting Lane

4

5

South Downs Way

South Downs Way

North Lane

Hoe La

Old
Hambledon
Cricket C

6

Newmans Fm

Lane

North Lane

Byden Copse

Hyden
Wood

7

Ditch
Acre Co

Lowton's
Copse

8

North Lane

A
North Fm
B
C
D
E

Little

North Lane

Bramble La
Clanfield
eld Lane

I grid square represents 500 metres

F   G   H   301   J   K

THE CAUS

B2070

Buriton
Business
Park

Hill

Greenway Lane

1

2

Clebe Road

Chalmes rd

Petersfield

Rd

Bones Lane

Heathfield

PH

High Street

Buriton CP School

PO

3

Kiln Lane

Ramsdean
Down

South La

271
▲
Butser Hill

Kiln La

Hangers Way

4

332

Limekiln
Lane

Newbarn Road

A3(T)

South Downs Way

Hangers Way

5

War Down

Head
Down Plantation

Queen Elizabeth Country Park

Hangers

Way

6

enbourne
wn

Hangers

Way

South Downs Way

Queen
Elizabeth
Forest

7

Staunton

Way

Holt
Down
Plantation

South Downs Way

Newbarn Road

8

Staunton

Way

que Lane

ne

F   G   H   361   J   K

Chalton
Down

332

302

331

362

A B C D E

Wrecks Lane

THE CAUSEWAY

B2070

A3

Buriton Business Park

Bolinge Hill Farm

Greenway

Lane

Nursted House

Cowhouse Farm

Crease Road

Bedstone Rd

Petersfield Rd

Bones Lane

North Lane

Pitcroft Lane

Heath

Buriton CP School

High Street

Buriton

Kiln Lane

Hangers Way

South La

Kiln La

New Rd

Hangers Way

South Downs Way

Coulters Dean Fm

South Downs Way

Sunwc

Head Down Plantation

Oakham Bottom

Downley

Hampshire County

West Sussex County

Newbarn Road

Mill

Ditcham Park Sch

Glass

Stanbridge

B2146

1 grid square represents 500 metres

308

A   B   C   D   E

Flood Street

Farm

A7
1 The Old Vineries
2 The Pantiles

Radnall Wood

I

B6
1 Allen Water Dr
2 Avon Meade
3 Cottage Ms
4 Garendon Ct
cont.

Peasash Farm

SP6

**Upper
Burgate**

2

B6(cont.)
5 Meadow Cl
6 Oaklands Cl
7 Pealsham Gdns
8 Ste Martin Gdns

Fryern Court Road

3

Fryern
Court

B7
1 Mill Ct
2 Vimoutiers Ct
3 Westgrove

4

Avon Valley Path

**Lower
Burgate**

337

Sandle
Dairy Farm

Lane

Puddletown

Fordingbridge
Junior &
Infant School

The
Burgate
School

Hertford

Dudley Av

Pennys

Burgate
Flds

5

Arch Farm
Industrial Est

B8
1 Bushells Farm
2 Diamond Cl

Marl Lane

Waverley Road

Georges Rd

Player

6

Sandle
Manor School

Marl Lane

Downwood

Willow Av

Orchard

C5
1 Bedford Cl
2 Burnham Rd
3 Merton Cl

Sandle Manor

Elmwood

Personage Park Dr

Picket La

Alexandra Rd

Alexandra Rd

Park Rd

FORDINGBRIDGE

7

Manor Farm Rd

Jubilee Rd

Station Road

Ashford
Close

Ashford

Victoria
Gdns

Station Road

Beechwood

Green La

Fordingbridge
Hospital

The
Bartons

P

Salisbury

A338

C6
1 Mayfly Cl
2 St Georges Crs

Ashford

Victoria
Road

Hotel

West St

Shaftesbury St

Council
Office

Town
Hall

HIGH ST

PROVOST ST

BRIDGE
ST

B3078

SOL

Cemetery

Stuckton Road

8

ROAD

BOWERWOOD

Padstow Pl

Lane

Mulberry
Gdns

CHURCH ST

Church
Farm

RINGWOOD
ROAD

County

A   B   C   D   E

366

Redbr

C7
1 The Bartons
2 Highbank Gdns
3 Moxhams
4 Orchard Gdns
5 Round Hl

C8
1 Brook Ter

Ditch

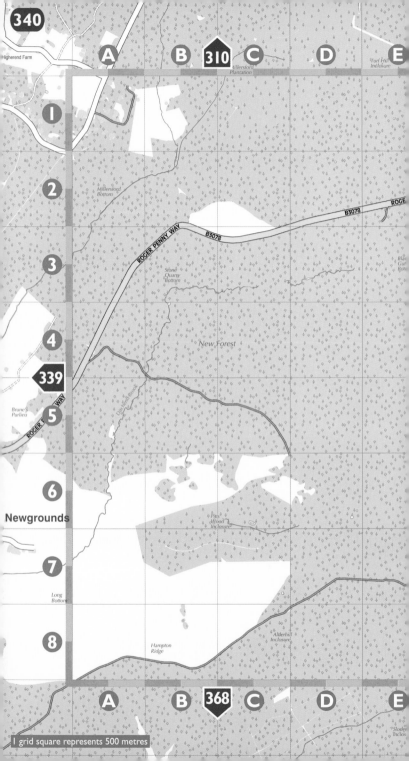

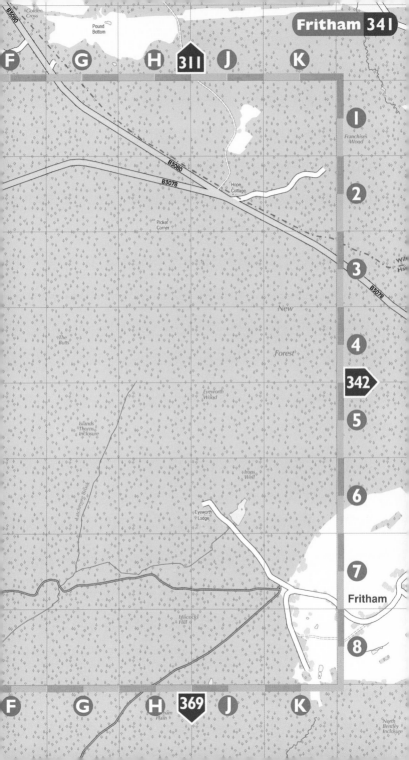

F G H **311** J K

1
Franchises
Wood

B3080

B3078

2

Hope
Cottage

Picket
Corner

3
B3078

Will
Ha

New

4

The
Butts

Forest

342

Eyeworth
Wood

5

Islands
Thorns
Inclosure

Ashstrops Brook

Irons
Well

6

Eyeworth
Lodge

7
Fritham

Hiscock's
Hill

8

F G H **369** J K

ham
Plain

North
Bentley
Inclosure

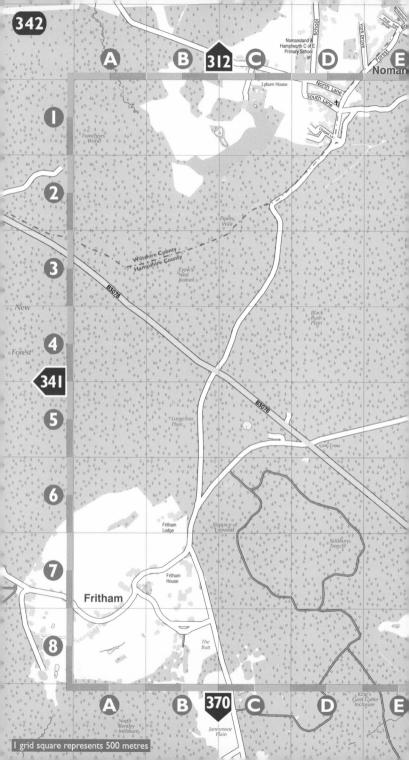

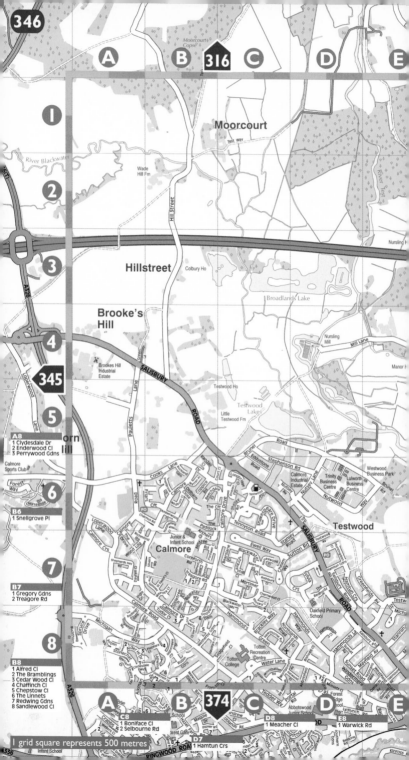

A · **B** · 316 · **C** · **D** · **E**

1

Moorcourts Copse

Moorcourt

2

River Blackwater

Tait Way

Wade Hill Fm

Hill Street

Nursling H

3

A326

Hillstreet

Colbury Ho

Broadlands Lake

Brooke's Hill

4

Nursling Mill

Mill Lane

Manor F

SALISBURY

345

Brookes Hill Industrial Estate

Pauletts Lane

Testwood Ho

Testwood Lakes

Little Testwood Fm

5

ROAD

A8
1 Clydesdale Dr
2 Enderwood Cl
3 Perrywood Gdns

orn
ill

Calmore Sports Club

Road

Road

Brunel

Folkestone Rd

Stephenson Rd

Calmore's Industrial Estate

Trinity Business Centre

Lulworth Business Centre

Westwood Business Park

Forest Way

Horseshoe

6

B6
1 Snellgrove Pl

Loperwood Lane

Calmore Cres

COOKS Lane

The Paddock

The Croft

Tennyson Road

Ewell Way

Blackwater

Sutton Road

Nutwood

Testwood

7

B7
1 Gregory Gdns
2 Treagore Rd

Junior & Infant School

Calmore

Comfrey Rd

Mortimer

SALISBURY ROAD

Oakfield Primary School

8

B8
1 Alfred Cl
2 The Bramblings
3 Cedar Wood Cl
4 Chaffinch Cl
5 Chepstow Cl
6 The Linnets
7 Redwing Gdns
8 Sandlewood Cl

Michigan Way

Calmore Road

Water Lane

Totton Recreation Centre

Totton College

Hammonds La

Green

Hammonds Cl

A326

A · **B** · 374 · **C** · **D** · **E**

C8
1 Boniface Cl
2 Selbourne Rd

School

D8
1 Meacher Cl

E8
1 Warwick Rd

RINGWOOD ROAD

Infant School

D7
1 Hamtun Crs

Abbotswood Junior School

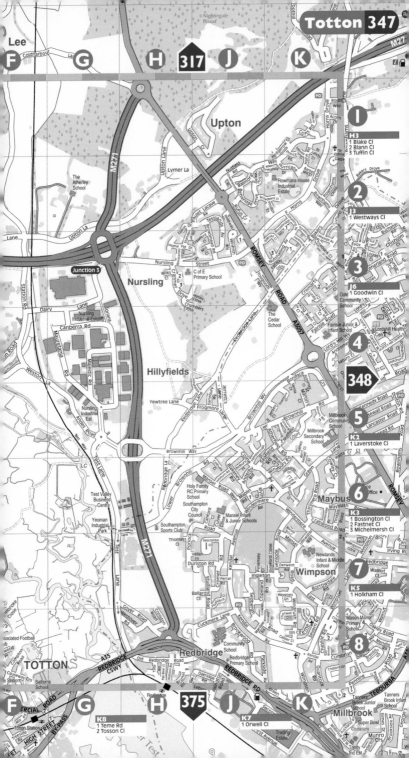

A8
1 Cateran Cl
2 Langdale Cl
3 Whernside Cl
4 Whitestone Cl

A7
1 Crabtree
2 Hawswater Cl

A3
1 Armstrong Ct
2 Blackbushe Cl
3 Colt Cl
4 Lucas Cl

318

A B C D E

C2
1 Brambling Cl

Rownhams

C8
1 Ashdene
2 Church St
3 Newman St
4 Regent's Gv
5 Settle Cl

D4
1 Bransbury Cl
2 Lyburn Cl
3 Purbrook Cl

347

Millbrook
Community
School

D6
1 Vinery Rd

aybush

D7
1 Didcot Rd
2 Newbury Rd
3 Vaudrey Cl

Wi ton

D8
1 Mayflower Rd
2 Victor St
3 Vincent's Gv

Lord's
Hill

Aldermoor

Coxford

Shirley
Warren

Old Shirley

WINCHESTER ROAD

Millbrook

E5
1 Lordswood Cl
2 Wolverley Ct

A B C D E

376

Shirley

E6
1 Fushsia Gdns
2 Lincoln Ct

E7
1 Cranbourne Cl

I grid square represents 500 metres

350

A B **320** C D E

B4
1 Alfred Rose Ct
2 Gilbury Cl
3 Grange Cl
4 Howard Cl
5 Lord Mtbatten Cl
6 Meadowside Cl
7 Pilgrim Pl
8 Westbrook Wy

A7
1 St Augustine Gdns
2 Saltmead

A8
1 Pettinger Gdns
2 Riverdene Pl

A3
1 Stoneham Cl
2 Summerfield Gdn

A4
1 Havenstone Wy
2 Rayners Gdns

C2
1 George Curl Wy

1

C5
1 Hillgrove Rd

C6
1 Lingfield Gdns
2 Longmead Rd

2

C7
1 Trent Cl

C8
1 Dalmally Gdns

3

D5
1 Creedy Gdns
2 Rostron Cl
3 Webburn Gdns

4

349

5

D6
1 Atlantic Park Vw
2 Benhams Rd
3 Camelia Gdns
4 Carpathia Cl
5 Gatcombe Gdns
6 Hallet Cl

6

D7
1 Benhams Farm Cl
2 Cleveland Ct
3 Grasdean Cl
4 Hazelwood Rd
5 Wakefield Ct

7

D8
1 Bramble Ms
2 Hood Rd
3 Macarthur Crs
4 Vanguard Rd

8

E5
1 Torridge Gdns

E6
1 Helford Gdns
2 Tresillian Gdns
3 Waldon Gdns

378

E7
1 Ennerdale Gdns
2 Grasmere Cl
3 Hedgerow Dr
4 Nomad Cl
5 Wheatcroft Dr

E8
1 Aberdour Cl
2 The Birches

North Stoneham

Southampton Airport Parkway Station

Southampton International Airport

Junction 5

Orion Business Centre

Swaythling

Hamp Park

SOUTHAMPTON

Bitterne Park

Townhill Park

Midanbury

A grid square represents 500 metres

Index callouts (right column):

1
G6
1 Hornbeam Gdns

2
G7
1 Caversham Cl
2 Glenlea Dr
3 Orchards Wy
4 Runnymede
5 Severn Wy
6 Warden Cl

3
G8
1 Chawton Cl
2 Leckford Cl
3 Roselands

4

352

5
H5
1 Brookside Wy

6
H6
1 Monarch Wy
2 Oakwood Ct
3 Willow Cl

7
H7
1 High St
2 Hildene Wy

8

Map labels:

West Horton Farm

Firtree Farm

Allington Manor Business Centre
Allington Manor Farm

Valley Park

Oaklands House

Winslowe House

Moorgreen Farm

M27

Cemetery

Primary School

Hornbeam Gdns

Hatch Bottom

Moorgreen

The Dro

Moorgreen Road

St James Primary School

Monarch Way

West End Surgery

Moorgreen Hospital

HIGH STREET

B3035

Tower Pl

Western Road

West

BOTLEY ROAD

M27

Wellington Pk

Nelson Ind Park

TOLLBAR WAY

West End

Hickley Farm

CHURCH HILL

B3035

Beechcroft

Minstead Av

Woodlands Community School

Harefield

Thornhill Park

Cheriton

THORNHILL PK RD

A27

MOORHILL

379

CHARLES WATTS WAY A334

Junction 7

UPPER

Water Industrial Est

Flanders Ind Park

S030

HEDGE END

Hedge End Retail Park

A   B   **332**   C   D   E

Cocburn Road

Class
Brow

itcham
ark Sch

1

Sussex Border Path

2

Ladyholt

Harris La.

Sussex Border Path

3

Woodcroft
Fm

PH

4

Sussex Border Path

361

5

Sussex Border Path

6

Idsworth
Down

Old
Idsworth Fm

7

Hampshire County
West Sussex County

Heberdens

8

Old
Idsworth

Markwells
Wood

A   B   **390**   C   D   E

I grid square represents 500 metres

336

A   B   C   D   E

Bull Hill Farm

Lopshill

Lower Daggons

Crendell

1

Pye Lane

Hart's Farm

more Farm

2

E2
1 Highwood Cl

HARE

DAGGONS

LANE

CRANBORNE ROAD

Daggons

Hare Lane Farm

3

King Barrow

Cripplestyle

Battenley Drove

4

Vale Acre Farm

Sleep Brook

Gotham

5

Cranborne
Common

t Heavy
e Centre

Telegraph
Plantation

6

Pistle
Down

7

Burrows Farm

Mount
Ararat

Boveridge
Heath

8

Burrows Lane

Stephen's
Castle

Wild Church
Bottom

Eastworth

Road

Finkenham

Road

Coopers Lane

Moorlands
Rd

Road

Coronation

Park Dr

The
Oaks

Berkeley
Cl

Moorlands
Road

ANDS RD

Police

wlands

A   **B**   **392**   **C**   **D**   **E**

Hillside County
First School

Stephen's La

BH31

ade Rd

Verwood
Town Council

Alderholt

Camel Green

I
G2
1 Lime Tree Cl

2
H2
1 Camel Green Rd
2 Down Lodge Cl
3 Fir Tree Hl
4 Silverdale Crs

3
H3
1 Ash Cl
2 Beech Cl
3 Bramble Cl
4 Hazel Cl
5 Saxon Wy

4

366

Bleak Hill

5
J2
1 Camel Green Rd
2 Gilbert Cl

Harbridge

6
J3
1 Kestrel Wy

7

8

Turmer

Lower Turmer

337

393

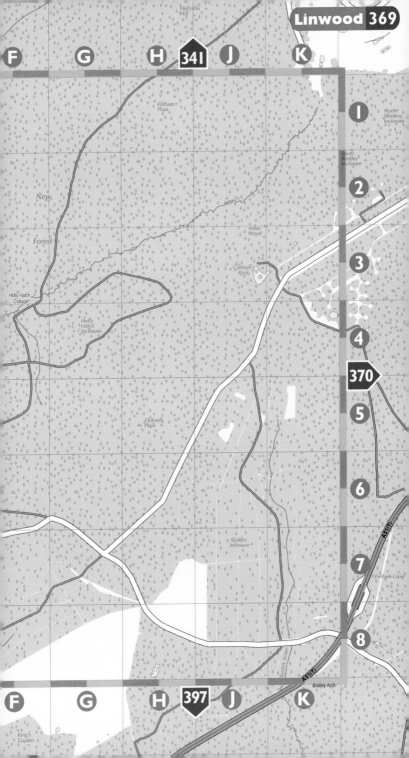

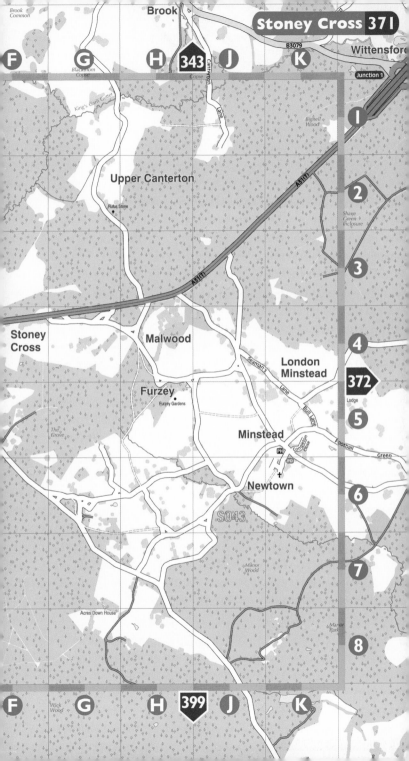

376

348

A7
1 Crooked Hays Cl
2 St Johns Ct

Millbrook

B2
1 Mottisfont Cl

Freemantle

S015

2

B7
1 Acorn Cl
2 The Limes
3 Malcroft Ms
4 Ripplewood
5 Tanglewood
6 Woodmoor Cl

3

C1
1 Endeavour Cl
2 Regent's Pk Gdns

City of Southampton
Hampshire County

4

River Test

375

5

C2
1 Victory Crs
2 Victory Sq
3 Waterhouse La

City of South
Hampshire Cou

Marchwood 6

D1
1 Beatrice Rd
2 May Rd

Cracknore
Hard

7

D2
1 Lakelands Dr

8

D6
1 Cracknore Hrd La

E1
1 Western Dist Cut

MARCHWOOD

404

E2
1 Princes Rd
2 Queenstown Rd

E3
1 Bridgwater Ct
2 Dymott Cl
3 Edith Haisman Cl

Marchwood
Priory
Hospital

I grid square represents 500 metres

A   B   C   D   E

1 grid square represents 500 metres

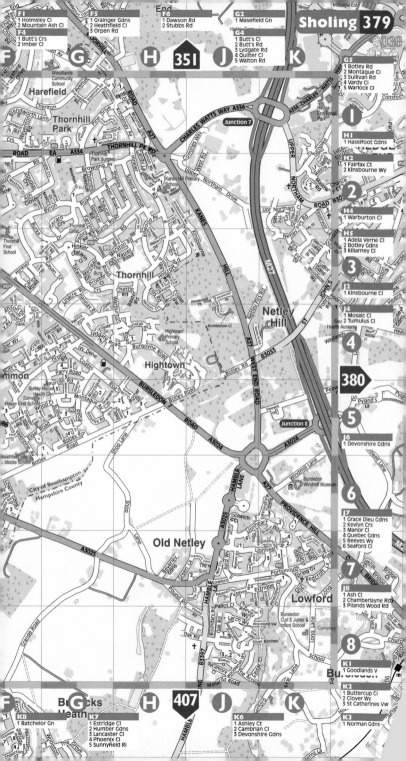

Sholing 379

F G H 359 J K

Old Mill Lane

The Crossways

Broadway Fm

Day Lane

New Road

Eastland Gate

Shrover

White Horse Lane

Edneys Lane

Anmore Lane

Broadway Lane

Amore Road

Anmore

Soake Road

Soake

Byngs Business Park

HAMBLEDON ROAD

B2150

Closewood Road

Mill Road

Maple Drive

Meadowlands Junior School

Woodcroft Lane

Meadowlands Infant School

Fulmer Walk

Partridge Gardens

Eagle Av

Puffin Wk

Magpie Wk

Kite Cl

Grebe Cl

Rachel Madocks School

Robin Gardens

Albretia

Hart Plain

Wecock

Chaplains Av

Kingscote Road

Sutton Road

Buckland

Silverdale Drive

Aiten Road

Sunnymead

Oaklands Grove

Maytree Gdns

Sunbury Cres

Sunny Field Cres

Fairfield

Purford Grove

Oak Cl

Hart

Cowplain School

MILTON ROAD

Hart Plain Av

Waterlooville Health Centre

Hart Plain Infant School

Hart Plain Junior School

Haslar

Crescent

Windsor Road

Bernina Av

Farm Grove

Tennyson

Crescent

Charlesworth Drive

Andrew

Margaret Road

Milton Road

Chaucer Cl

Old Park Farm

Waterberry Drive

Churchill Yard Industrial Est

Rowlands Av

Wallis Road

Queen's Road

Aston

Westside Vw

Elder Cl

Silverthorne Way

Relay Rd

Jubilee Road

Winifred Rd

Charminster Cl

Waterlooville Football Club

Jubilee Business Cen

Hambrook Road

Maurepas Road

Aysgarth Road

LONDON ROAD A3M

WATERLOO

Maurepas

Queen's Rd

MAUREPAS WAY

Bramley Rd

Hulbert Road

B2150

Cavendish

Cemetery

Pipers Wood Ind Park

Plant Farm

Spur Rd

Hulbert Road

The Waterloo School

Warfield Av

1
F5
1 Upper Piece

2
H6
1 Bernina Cl

Lovedean

Coldhill Lane
Tiford Road
The Curve
Whichers
Yoells Lane
Gypsy Lane

3
J5
1 Sutton Cl

James
Eagle Av
Flag Wk

4
Milton Road
Keats Rd

388

Longwood Av
Forest Close

5
J7
1 Armstrong Cl
2 Charlesworth Dr
3 The Hundred
4 Petersham Cl

Purley Cl
Linda
Silvester
Close Lawrence Av
Berg Rd
Aaron Cl

6
K4
1 Kingfisher Cl
2 Thrush Wk

Avenue
Hart Plain

7
K5
1 Chatburn Av
2 Chesterton Gdns
3 Maytree Rd
4 Newbolt Cl
5 Shakespeare Gdn

8

K6
1 Fairbourne Cl
2 Homer Cl
3 Wedgewood Wy

A B 362 C D E

1

2 Finchdean

3 Deanlane End

389

5

6 Rowland's Castle

7

8

West

Old
Id

Markwells
Wood

Ashcroft
La

South
Holt Fm

Northwood
Fm

Forests

Warren
Down

Drews Fm

Stansted Forest

Hare
Warren

Wellsworth

Wellsworth La

Rowlands
Castle Station
Surgery

English
Gallery

Horsepasture Fm

Holme Farm

Stubbermere

Sussex Border Path

Monarch's Way

Monarch's Way

Sussex Border Path

Sussex Border Path

Dean Lane

Finchdean Rd

Finchdean Rd

Sussex Border Path

Manor Road Lane

Woodhouse

Boxes

The Fairway

The Peak with

Hillis with

Broadmere Cl

Uplands

Finchdean Rd

College

Drift

Woodberry La

Clay Dr

ID B2148

COMLE

LC

A B 418 C D E

392

A   B   364   C   D   E

Stephen's Castle

Burrows Lane

Boveridge Heath

Eastworth Road

Edmondsham Rd

Church Bottom

Cooper's Lane

Moorlands Rd

Park Dr

Pinkeley

ANDS RD

The OAKS

lands

1
A1
1 Manor Wy

Police

RINGWOOD

Hillside County First School

BH31

Verwood Town Council

ROAD

Strathmore Dr

Howard Rd

Newtown Road

Compton Close

2
A2
1 Manor Ct
2 Manor Gdns
3 Pennine Wy

Oaklands

B3072

VERWOOD

Verwood Leisure Centre

Burdens La

Shard Close

Crescent Rd

Verwood Industrial Est

Verwood Sports Gen

Noel Hill

Southernhay Rd

The Cha

Manor Road Surgery

Chiltern Drive

Valiant Drive

BLACK

Sandy Lane

B3081

The Cha...

3
A3
1 Cotswold Cl
2 Mendip Cl
3 Purbeck Dr
4 St Michaels Cl
5 Woodpecker Cl

DALEH

Keswick

Pennine Wy

MANOR ROAD

B3072

Burnbake

Belmont Rd

Foxes Close

Owls Road

Newtown Road

Paddock Gv

Meadow

Lombardy

Moneyfly

Fairwood Wy

Laburnum

The Chase

Saunters

The Forestside

Roseberry Close

Cemetery

4

River Crane

Michaels Lane

Spring Close

Summer Flds

Howe Lane

St

Michaels Road

Lake The Surgery

Claylake Dr

Bingham Road

Lake Road

Woodlinken Drive

Burn Dr

Burn Cl

Hazel

Wisteria Ave

Magnolia

Woodlinken

Brunel Cl

Forest Cl

Ebblake Indust Est

Bessemer Close

5
B1
1 Starlight Farm Cl

Manor Farm

Potterne

River Crane

Way

6 b Orchard
Crab Orchard Way
ROAD
B2
1 Acorn Wy
2 Heathlands Cl
3 Oaks Mead
4 Shires Mead

VERWOOD

B3072

7
B3
1 Nightingale Cl
2 Orchard Ct

Doctors Surgery

Church

Lower Common

8 Three Legged Cross

RINGWOOD ROAD

Fern Bank

Dymewood Rd

Ringwood Road

Magpies Sports Club

WEST MOORS ROAD

A   B   420   C   D   E

Woolsbridge

Lwr Common

Ringwood Road

C2
1 Foxhills
2 Noon Hill Dr

D3
1 Lavender Cl

School

I grid square represents 500 metres

Plumley Wood

F **G** **H** 365 **J** **K**

Harbridge School
Turmer

Plumley Farm

Harefield Plantation

I Lower Turm

Turmer Brook

Home Farm
Shepherds Lane

2

Chesyl Mill

Nea Drive

3

Ringwood Forest

Avenue

Somerley Park

4

Somerley

Rea Drive

394

B3081

5

Ashley Drive

Doveshayes Drive

6

Hampshire County
Dorset County

Ashley Farm

Moors Valley Country Park

7

VERWOOD ROAD B3081

Baker's Hanging

Ashley Drive

8

F **G** **H** 421 **J** **K**
Watchr Wood

B3081

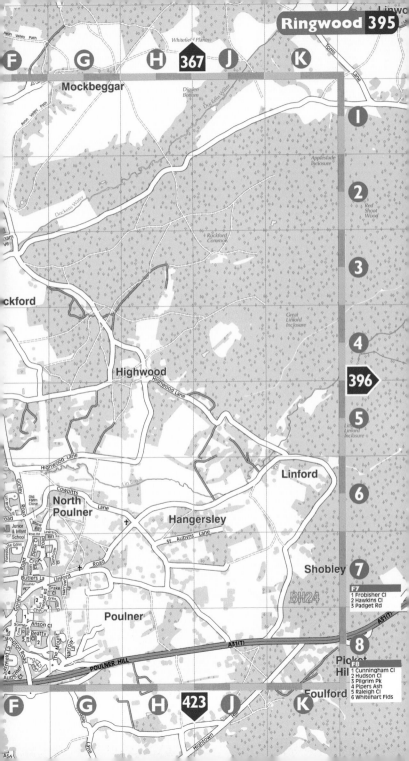

367

F **G** **H** **J** **K**

Linwood

1

2

3

4

396

5

6

7

8

Mockbeggar

Whitefield Plantn

Diggen Bottom

Ox Eyes Water

Avon Valley Path

Avon Valley Path

Appleslade Inclosure

Red Shoot Wood

Dockens Water

Rockford Common

ckford

Great Linford Inclosure

Highwood

Highwood Lane

Little Linford Inclosure

Highwood Lane

Linford

Cowpitts Lane

Lin Brook

North Poulner

Old Farm Close

Hangersley

St Aubyns Lane

Shobley

F7
1 Frobisher Cl
2 Hawkins Cl
3 Padget Rd

BH24

Poulner

Anson Cl

Beatty

The Mount

Narrow

POULNER HILL

A31(T)

A31(T)

Picket Hill

F8
1 Cunningham Cl
2 Hudson Cl
3 Pilgrim Pk
4 Pipers Ash
5 Ralegh Cl
6 Whitehart Flds

Foulford

F **G** **H** **J** **K**

423

Hightown

ASA

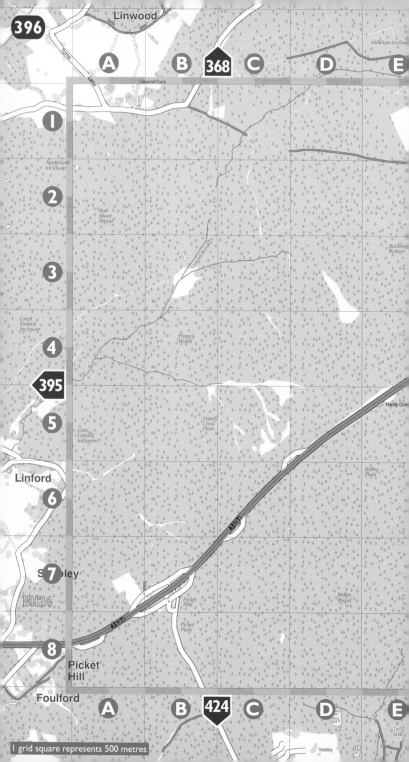

396

Linwood

A   B   368   C   D   E

Milkham Inclose

1

Linwood Farm

Appleslade
Inclosure

2

Red
Shoot
Wood

Buckher
Bottom

3

Linford Brook

Great
Linford
Inclosure

4

Pinnick
Wood

395

5

Little
Linford
Inclosure

Handy
Cross
Plain

Handy Cro

Ridley
Plain

Linford

6

A31(T)

S   ley

7

BH24

Picket
Post

Ridley
Wood

A31(T)

Picket
Plain

8

Picket
Hill

Foulford

A   B   424   C   D   E

Turf
Cro

Vereley

I grid square represents 500 metres

F G H 369 J K

I

2

B

3

4

398

5

6

7

8

F G H 425 J K

Bratley Water

A31(T)

Bratley Arch

King's Garden

Bratley Inclosure

Bratley Wood

Backley Bottom

Backley Inclosure

New

Forest

ackley
ain

Soarley Beeches

North Oakley Inclosure

Beech Bed Inclosure

Harvest Slade Bottom

Old House

Berry Beeches

Burley Otter Rails Inclosure

Berry Wood

South Oakley Inclosure

Burley Lodge

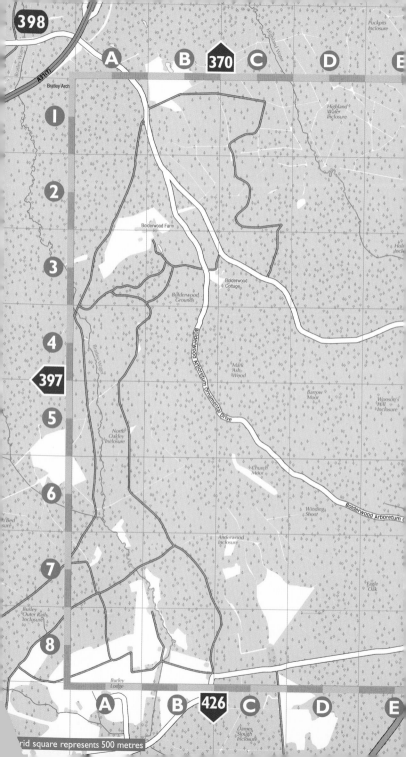

A

B

C

D

E

Puckpits
Inclosure

Bratley Water

A31(T)

Bratley Arch

Highland Water

I

Highland
Water
Inclosure

2

Bolderwood Farm

Hol
Incl

3

Bolderwood
Cottage

Bolderwood
Grounds

Bratley Water

4

Mark
Ash
Wood

Barrow
Moor

Wooson's
Hill
Inclosure

5

North
Oakley
Inclosure

6

Church
Moor

h Bed
sure

Bolderwood Arboretum

Winding
Shoot

7

Eagle
Oak

Bratley
Outer Rails
Inclosure

8

Anderwood
Inclosure

Burley
Lodge

A

B

C

D

E

Dames
Slough
Inclosure

Bolderwood Ornamental Drive

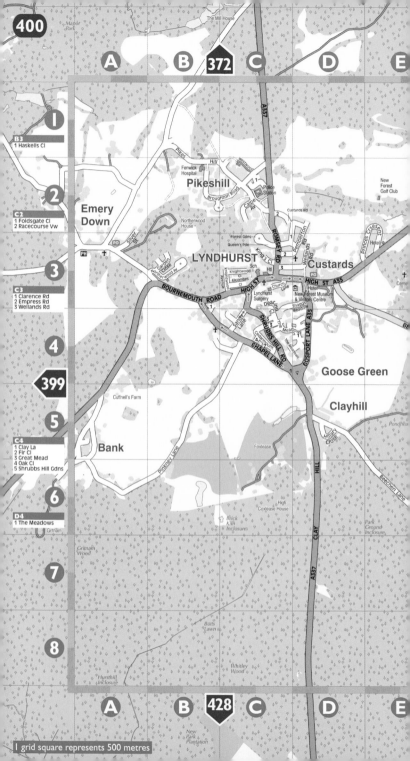

A B 372 C D E

1

2

3

4

399

5

6

7

8

Manor Park
The Mill House

Fenwick Hospital
Pikeshill
Police Station

Emery Down
Northerwood House

New Forest Golf Club

Hotel

Forest Gdns
Queen's Pde

LYNDHURST
knightwood
Elcombes Cl

Custards
Custards Rd

HIGH ST A35
New Forest Museum & Visitors Centre
Lyndhurst Surgery

BOURNEMOUTH ROAD

CHAPEL LANE
SHRUBBS HILL RD.
GOSPORT LANE A35

Goose Green

Clayhill

Cuffnell's Farm

Bank

Foxlease

Pinmey Lane

CLAY HILL

BEECHEN LANE

High Coxlease House

Brick Kiln Inclosure

Gritnam

Gritnam Wood

Butts Lawn

Whitley Wood

Hurshill Inclosure

Hursthill Inclosure
Park Ground Inclosure

A B 428 C D E

New Park Plantation

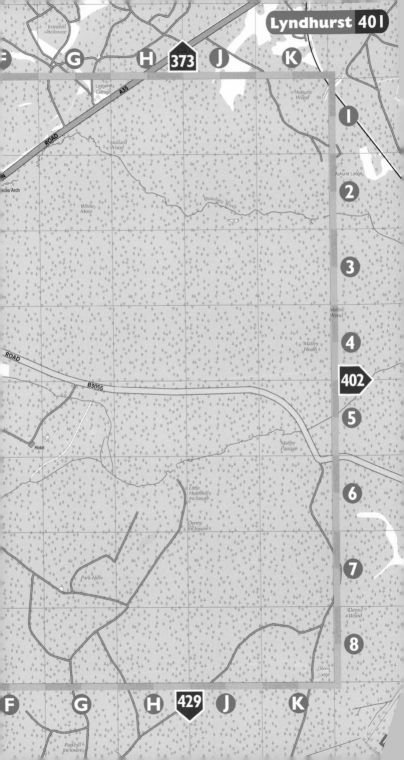

373

F G H J K

I

2

3

402

4

5

6

7

8

F G H 429 J K

Ironshill Inclosure

Lodgehills Cottage

A35

ROAD

Mallard Wood

ces Arch

White Moor

Beaulieu River

Ashurst Wood

Ashurst Lodge

Matley Wood

Matley Heath

ROAD

B3056

Hotel

Matley Passage

Little Holmhill Inclosure

Denny Inclosure

Park Hill

Denny Wood

Denny Lodge

Parkhill Inclosure

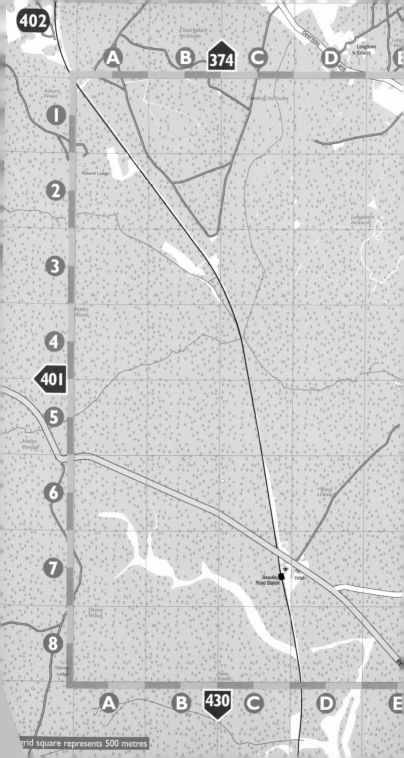

F   **G**   **H**   375   **J**   **K**

MARCHWOOD

Marchwood
C of E
Infant School

Hythe Road

Lane

Stapewood

Arters   Lawn

Twiggs Lane

End

Lane

Twiggs

Foxhill Farm

Beaulieu Road

Birchlands Farm

Collier's Lane

I

2

3

4

404

5

6

7

8

Ipley
Inclosure

Ipley
Manor

Yew
Tree
Heath

Beaulieu River

King's
Hat
Inclose

Ferny
Crofts

F   **G**   **H**   431   **J**   **K**

404

A MARCHWOOD

B **376** **C** **D** **E**

Marchwood
C of E
Infant School

Willow

Pumpfield Farm

Year's Lane

1

Marchwood
Priory
Hospital

A326

Main Road

BYPASS

Church Farm Cotts

Lock's Farm

D4
1 Broomy Cl
2 Eyeworth Wk
3 Magnolia Cl
4 Vaughan Rd

2

Odn City

Church Farm

Dibden

D5
1 Ridgewood Cl
2 Rockram Gdns
3 Rooksbridge
4 Roundcopse

Birchlands Farm

3

The Old Manor

D6
1 Downwood Cl

4

403

Marchwood
Inclosure

Manor Road

HYTHE BYPASS

Applemore

A326

Boxley Cy

Clavells

After Way

Challenger

Chevit

Morton Avenue

Cumberland Way

5

Exter Way

Claypits La

Applemore
Recreation
Centre

Oak Lodge
School

Capel Dr

Cyprus Gdns

Redwood

Canterbury Dr

Challenge

E5
1 Ashburton Cl
2 The Brackens
3 Capella Gdns
4 Cotswold Cl
5 Moorland Cl
6 The Sylvans

6

Applemore
College

Roman Rd

Beechwood Wy

Alder

Milne Cl

Oakenbrow

Carisbrooke

Way

E6
1 Blackdown Cl
2 Brendon Cl
3 Mendip Gdns
4 Pentland Cl
5 The Quantocks

7

Buchan
Ct

Lewis Ct

Oaklands

**Dibden
Purlieu**

E7
1 Roman Gdns

8

HYTHE BY-PASS

Roman Rd

Nash

The
Noads

Dibden
Inclosure

King's
Hat
Inclosure

A **B** **432** **C** **D** **E**

Crabbat
Inclosure

8
1 Laburnum Crs
2 Maple Rd

Beaulieu
Heath

I grid square represents 500 metres

F6
1 Marlborough Ct

F7
1 Haynes Wy
2 Woodlands Ct

G5
1 Boundstone
2 Conifer Cl
3 Hawthorn Rd
4 Midway
5 Tormead

G6
1 Badgers Wk
2 Byeways
3 Drakes Cl
4 Forest Hill Wy
5 Heathfield
6 Noads Cl

G7
1 Chaveney Cl
2 Hartley Wk
3 Lambourne Cl
4 Ratcliffe Rd
5 Windmill Copse

G8
1 Corbould Rd

H3
1 Mount House Cl

H4
1 Alexandra Cl
2 Carpenter Cl
3 Court House Cl
4 Drummond Rd
cont.

H4(cont.)
5 Fairfield Cl
6 Green Cl
7 Mariners Ms
8 Pylewell Rd

H5
1 Abbey Cl
2 Coat Gdns
3 Freedom Ct

H6
1 Frayslea
2 Greatwood Cl
3 Knightstone Gra
4 Langd'wn Lwn Cl
5 Rose Cl

H7
1 Andrew Cl
2 Buttercup Cl
3 Butts Ash La
4 Chaloner Crs
cont.

H7(cont.)
5 Hartley Cl
6 Ingle Gln
7 Northbourne Cl
8 Silvers End

H8
1 Devonshire Gdns
2 Stokesay Cl

J4
1 Sir Christopher Cl

F6
1 Furzedown Ms
2 Hamilton Ms

G6
1 Pinewood Crs
2 Spinney Gdns
3 Tates Rd

J5
1 Tates Rd

HYTHE

Langdown

Frostlane

Buttsash

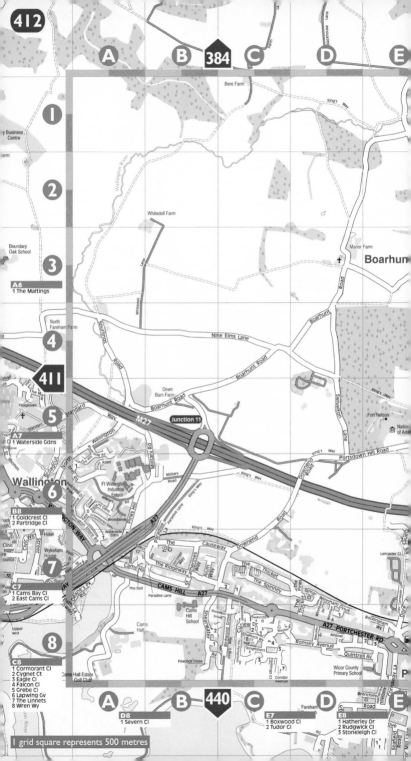

Three
Legged Cr... **A** **B** 392 **C** **D** **E**

Magpies
Sports
Club

RINGWOOD ROAD

Fern Bank

Dymewood Rd

Ringwood Road

I

Woolsbridge

Ringwood Road

Ashley Heath
Industrial Est

River

2

A5
1 Bridges Cl

Crane
Way

Woolsbridge
Industrial Est

Victory Cl

Woolsbridge Small
Business Centre

Liberty Cl

Azura Cl

Wools Bridge

Horton Road

Ringwood Rd

33072

Payne Cl

3

Gundymoor
Trading
Estate

A7
1 Canterbury Cl
2 Shaftesbury Rd

Old
Barn

Casteman Tramway

Pine
La...

4

Castleman Tramway

Moors River

Hill
Way

Garth Cl
Heath

Rowan Cl

Willow Cl
Conifer
Cl
Rd

Sarum

Sarum
Avenue

Sarum Av

5

Castleman Tramway

Moorlands Rise

West
Moors
Plantation

Moors River

Oaks

B7
1 Heatherdown Rd
2 Heatherdown Wy

Fir Cl

Glenwood

Moortla...

Glenwood Way

6

Belle Vue Grove

Oakhurst
Lane

Uplands Road

Uplands
Rd

East Moors
Farm

Fir Cl

RINGW

E3
1 Forest Edge Cl

WEST MOORS

Avon Cl

7

Woolsbepe

Heatherlea Way

West Moors
Middle School

Southern Avenue

Maloren Wy

Uplands

RINGWOOD RD

RINGWOOD ROAD

St Leonards
Hospital

A31(T)

Bo...

33072

8 A31(T)

A31(T)

RINGWOOD RD

A **B** 452 **C** **D** **E**

RINGWOOD ROAD

Trickett's Cross

Ford Cl

Ford

Martins Wy

Moors Rv

1 grid square represents 500 metres

F **G** **H** 393 **J** **K**

1

B3081

F5
1 Cedar Av
2 Garden-lane

2

Castleman Trailway

Watchmoor Wood

Farm Lane
Folly

Ringwood Waldorf School

Horton Road

G2
1 High St

Ashley

Warren Dr
Green Acres
Warren Cl
Warren Cl

3

Castleman's Way

David's Ln

H3
1 Compton Bchs

The Close

St Ives Wood

Struan Gardens
Struan Dr
Foxley Park
Struan Court
The Beeches

Horton Rd
Peveril Cl

Ashley Heath

Ashley Drive W

St Ives CP School
St Ives Park
Sandy Lane
Fernbank

Whitfield Park

St Ives

4

Hurn Road

The Avon

5

422

H4
1 The Close
2 Greenwood Cps

Barnsfield Road

Windmill Lane
Windmill Cl

Egmont
Egmont
Egmont

6

H5
1 Russell Gdns

Egmont Gdns

Dorset County
Hampshire County

A31(T) RINGWOOD ROAD

Avon Heath Country Park

Barnsfield Road

Point Park Road

A338 Hurn Road

Alder School

Leybrook Common

7

River Avon

Boundary La

Boundary Lane

Foxbury Road

Foxbury Road

Grange Estate

8

Matcham's House

Matcham's Park

A31(T)

eonards

F **G** **H** 453 **J** **K**

422

394

A B 394 C D E

RINGWOOD

1

421

2

C1
1 Centre Pl
2 The Close
3 Cottage Ms
4 High St
5 Kings Arms Rw
6 Meeting Ho La
7 The Sweep

Ashley

3

D1
1 Bishop Ct
2 Clark's Cl
3 Frampton Pl
4 Middle La
5 Mount Pleasant
6 The Quomp

4

421

5

D2
1 Charing Cl
2 Duck Island La
3 Harry Barrow Cl
4 Nursery Rd
cont.

6

D2(cont.)
5 Southfield
6 Southfield Ms
7 Victoria Gdns
8 Waterloo Wy
9 Woodstock La

7

E2
1 Coniston Rd

8

Moortow

Kingston

A B 454 C D E

1 grid square represents 500 metres

Poulner

A31(T)

POULNER HILL

395

Picket
Hill

Foulford

I

2

Novan Lane

Hightown Hill

Hightown

Hightown Road

Hightown Hill

Forest Lane

Forest Lane

Hurn Farm

Lakeside

Merlin

3

Vales
Moor

Wood End Rd

Forest Edge Rd

Knaves
Ash

Crow
Hill
Top

Crow

Barrack Lane

4

Strodgemoor
Bottom

424

Charles's Lane

5

Charles's Lane

6

ingston
Great
Common

Bagnum Farm

7

8

Sandford

455

Bisterne
Common

F   G   H   J   K

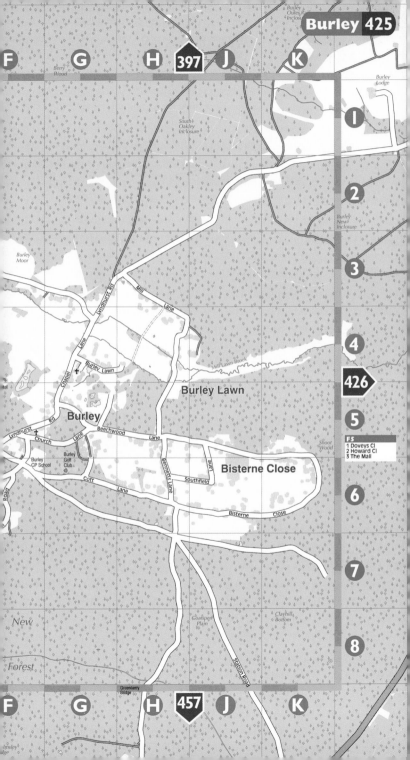

F G H 397 J K

1

2

3

4

426

5

F5
1 Doveys Cl
2 Howard Cl
3 The Mall

6

7

8

Berry Wood

South Oakley Inclosure

Burley Lodge

Burley New Inclosure

Burley Moor

Lyndhurst Rd

Mill Lane

Chapel Lane

Burley Lawn

Mill Lawn Brook

Burley Lawn

Burley

Lyndhurst Rd

Church Lane

Beechwood Lane

Shoot Wood

Burley CP School

Burley Golf Club

Bennetts Lane

Bisterne Close

Burn

Southfield

Cott Lane

Bisterne Close

New

Forest

Goatspen Plain

Clayhill Bottom

Station Road

Greenberry Bridge

Insley Idge

F G H 457 J K

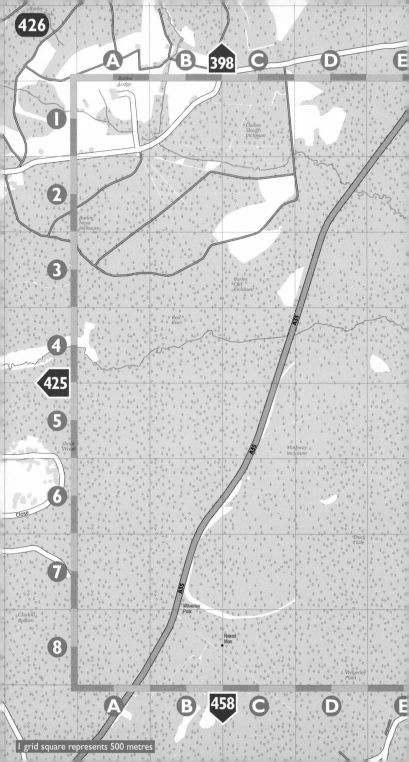

426

A   B   398   C   D   E

1   Burley
     Lodge

Dames
Slough
Inclosure

2   Burley
     New
     Inclosure

3   Burley
     Old
     Inclosure

Red
Rise

4

◀ 425

5   Shoot
     Wood

Madway
Inclosure

6

Close

Duck
Hole

7

Clayhill
Bottom

A35

Wilverley
Post

8

Naked
Man

Wilverley
Plain

A   B   458   C   D   E

1 grid square represents 500 metres

F G H **399** J K

I

2

3

4

428

5

6

7

8 South Weirs

F G H **459** J K

New Forest

Fletchers Thorns Inclosure

Vinney Ridge Inclosure

Rhinefield Ornamental Drive

Poundhill Inclosure

Poundhill Heath

Black Water

Ober Heath

Hotel

Aldridgehill Inclosure

White Water

Beachern Wood

Ober Water

Crab Tree Earth

Ober House

The Coppice

Whitemoor Road

New Forest Drive

North Weirs

White Moor

Five Thorns Hill

Hinchelsea Moor

Burley Road

South Weirs

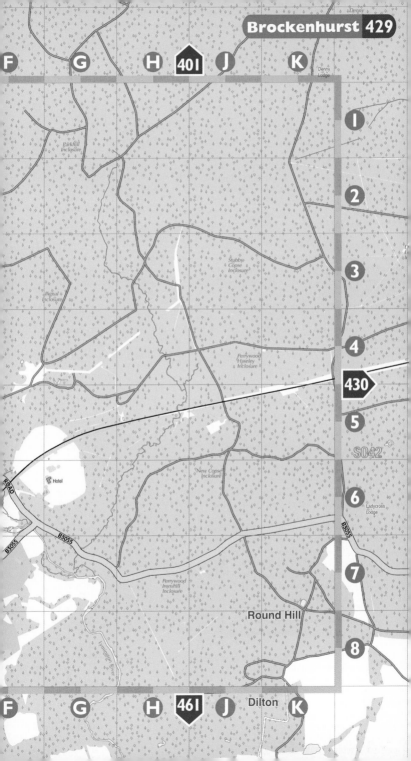

F G H 401 J K

1
2
3
4
430
5
S042
6
7
8

Denny
Denny Lodge

Parkhill Inclosure

Stubby Copse Inclosure

Signal Inclosure

Perrywood Haseley Inclosure

Hotel

ROAD

B3055

B3055

B3053

New Copse Inclosure

Ladycross Lodge

Perrywood Ironshill Inclosure

Lymington River

Round Hill

F G H 461 J Dilton K

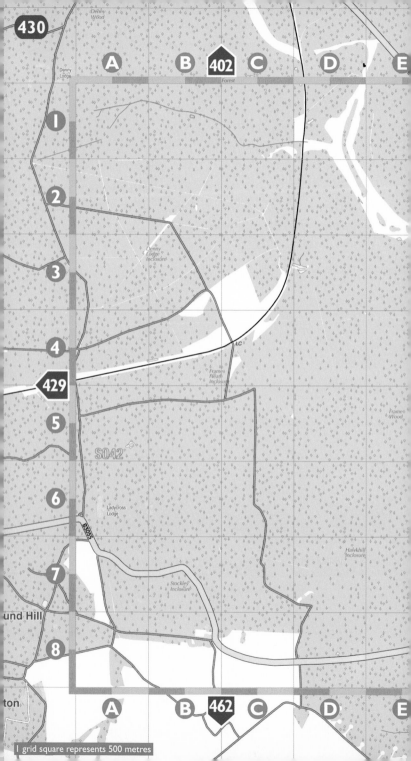

430

A   B   402   C   D   E

Denny
Wood

Denny
Lodge

Forest

1

2

Denny
Lodge
Inclosure

3

4   LC

429   Frame
                                 Heath
                                 Inclosure

5   Frame
                                                            Wood

SO42

6   LadyCross
         Lodge

B3055

7   Stockley
               Inclosure

und Hill   Hawkhill
                                              Inclosure

8

ton

A   B   462   C   D   E

1 grid square represents 500 metres

Buttsash

F G H **405** J K

Crete

Lunedale Rd
Heatherstone
Ashwood
Hawley
Monks Wk
Beverley Road
Butts Ash La
Buttsash Avenue
Ashleigh Cl
Fleur de Lys
Fawley Road
Beach Crs
Holly Close
Laburnum Ct
Cedar
Fonsley Rd
Hardley La
New
Fawley Road

Fawley
Inclosure

HYTHE
BY-PASS A326
Solent Wy

New Rd

Roman Rd
Old School La
A326

Hardley

Chevron Business Park
The Mill Pond
Harrier Wy
Lime Kiln Lane
Main Rd
Copthorne Pk Esto
LONG

Sycamore Dr
Larch Av
Hardley School

Little Holbury

Manor Infant School

Link
Lime Kiln Lane
Park Lane

'Holbury Purlieu

Larksbur Gdns
Wedgewood
Southbourne Avenue
Nor Close

Manor Road
Holbury
DROVE
Watton Rd
Romsey Rd
Ansley Rd
Stanley Rd
Will

Stonyford Pond

434
Ho

School
Bower
Studio
Broadok
Sedrise
Eastcot
Cl Elms
Moat
Fourcott Dr
White
Cares
Cross Roewood
Brambla
Myve
Cl
Rollestone Road
William

Rollestone Farm

LONG LANE
PO

I

2

3

4

5

Rollestone Rd

6

7

Rowndown

Stock Water

Kings Copse Inclosure

King's Copse

Blackwell Common

8

Steeple Copse
Summer Lane

F G H **465** J K

Langle

Charnwo

436

Hamble Spit **A**

B **408** **C** Hook with Warsash Primary School **D** **E**

Bevis Cl
Osborne Rd
Church Rd
Spruce Cl
New Rd
New Rd

Newtown

Hook

Hook Park Rd

I

2

Hook Park

Cowes Lane

Solent Drive

Workman's Lane

3

Chilling Lane

Solent Way

Workman's La

4

ISLE OF WIGHT

◀**435**

5

6

Calshot Castle

7

8

A **B** **C** **D** **E**

I grid square represents 500 metres

Common

Abshot

F   G   H   409   J   K   Titchfield

Hook La

Hookgate Coppice

Occupation Lane

Posbrook Lane

Brownwich Lane

Singledge

Little
Posbrook

Triangle Lane

Brownwich Lane

Brownwich Farm

438

River Meon

Meon

Solent Way

Titchfield
Haven

Cliff   Hill
Road

F   G   H   J   K

1
2
3
4
5
6
7
8

Rosedale Cl
Garstons Cl
Coach
The Cl
Bellfield
Hewett Road   Lwr Bellfield
Heyett
Gardner Road

F
TER

G

H

413

J

HAMPTON ROAD

K

I

2

3

4

442

5

Tipner

6

7

8

F

G

H

470

J

K

F1
1 Gladstone Gdns

F8
1 Alencon Cl
2 Kynon Cl

Portsmouth Harbour

Whale
Island

Horsea Is

Tipner Lane

Church Rd
Portchester
Castle

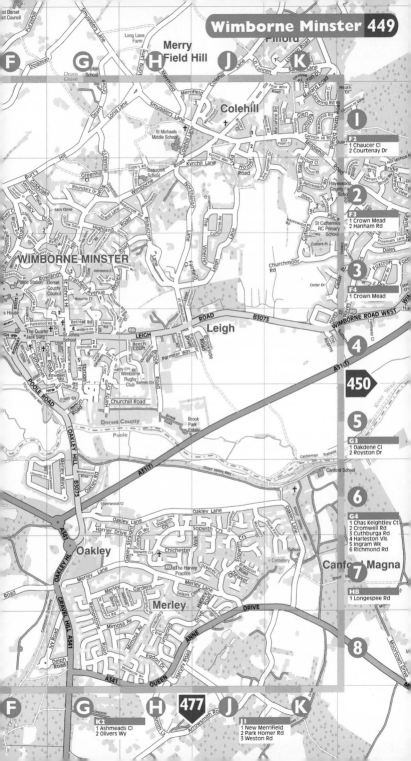

A   B   C   D   E

1

A1
1 Cannon Hill Gdns

Cannon Hill Plantation

Ferndown Stour and Forest Trail

2

A2
1 Canford View Dr

Hayeswood
County First
School

RC Primary
School

3

Churchmoor
Rd

B2
1 Hunter Cl
2 Saddle Cl
3 Spur Cl
4 Suffolk Cl

WIMBORNE RD W

Martindale Av

WIMBORNE ROAD WEST

Ham La.

Stapehill

Stapehill Abbey

Keeble's Lane

Wimborne Road West

Wetlands
Avenue

Castleman Trailway

HAM LANE

Fox's Lane

4

A31(T)

449

**Little
Canford**

old
Ham
Lane

Fox's
Close

B3073

HAM

LANE

Stapehill Road

5

River Stour

Castleman Trailway

Hampreston
Primary
School

Canford School

6

Oakley Lane

Hampreston

7

Canford Magna

Stour Valley Way

8

Moortown Drive

Moortown Farm

Stour Valley Way

River Stour

Dorset County
Poole

MAGNA

478

ROAD

Knig

Knighton

A   B   C   D   E

A31(T)

F G H J K

I
F2
1 Barrow Vw

2
H3
1 Old School Cl

3
H5
1 Heath Farm Cl

4

452

5
J2
1 Bramley Rd

Lone Pine Way

6
J5
1 Brune Wy
2 Glenmoor Rd
3 Wincombe Cl

7
K6
1 Amberwood
2 Garden Wk

Parley Sports Club

CHRISTCHURCH

West Parley

8

FERNDOWN

BH22

Ferndown Upper School

Ferndown Sports Centre

Ferndown Town Council

Ferndown Middle School

Ferndown First School

Ferndown Medical Centre

East Dorset Area Health Authority

NEW ROAD

RINGWOOD ROAD

VICTORIA ROAD

WIMBORNE RD E

WEST MOORS RD

B3072

A348

A347

Longham

Dudsbury

CHRISTCHURCH ROAD B3073

Holmwood

River Stour

K8
1 Elm Tree Wk
2 Longfield Dr

K3
1 Pringles Cl

Ensbury Bridge

Parley Cross

454

422

453

482

Bisterne

Avon

Hurn Road

A338

Lane

A338

River Avon

Week Farm

Week Common

Avon Common

Pithouse Farm

Princes Lane

Causeway

Avon Causeway

A338

Sopley Common

Dragon Lane

Path

B3347

Avon Valley Path

Upper Bisterne F

Bisterne Manor

Lower Bisterne Farm

Anna Lane

Hotel

Avon Tyrrell Farm

London   Lane

London   Lane

Avon Valley Path

B3347

River Avon

Court Farm

B3347 RINGWOOD

ROAD

Meadow Cl

Lane

Avon Valley Path

A

B

C

D

E

1

2

3

4

5

6

7

8

A

B

C

D

E

I grid square represents 500 metres

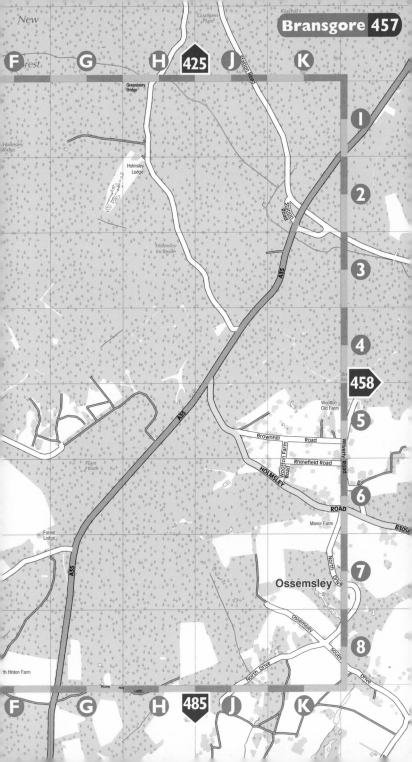

South Weirs

F G H `427` J K

I

2

3

4

`460`

5

6

7

8

White Moor

Five Thorns Hill

Flinches Moor

Burley Road

Hincheslea Wood

Long Slade Bottom

Set Thorns Inclosure

Cemetery

Burley Road

Blackhamsley Ho

Widden Bottom

Durns Tow

J6
1 Highfield Gdns

Mead End

Adlam's Lane

Mead End Road

Brighton Road

Oakenbrow

Manchester Road

Station Road

Middle Road

Anderwood

Cruse Cl

Hotel

Jordans Lane

Widden

Thorns Rd

B3055

DURNSTOWN

Back Lane

Set

Hyde

Sway
Sway Station

The Gallery

The Surg

Sway St Lukes Primary Schools

Sway Park Industrial Estate

Hotel

Church Lane

Jubilee Court

Birchy Hill

BIRCHY HILL

B3055

Chapel Lane

Coombe Lane

Broadley House

Lower Mead End Road

Avon Water

South Sway Lane

King's Farm

Arnewood Manor

Pauls

F G H `487` J K

Crabbswood Lane

ARNEWOOD BRIDGE

Linnies Lane

Barrows La

South Weirs

Burley Road

A **B** 428 **C** **D** **E**

Primary School
Avenue Rd
Partridge Rd
Highwood Road
The Surgery
Tattenham Rd
Brockenhurst Station
Church Lane

1

SWAY

Wick

South

2

Blackhamsley Ho
Brockenhurst Manor Golf Club

Tattenham Lane

Setley

LYMINGTON ROAD

Tilebarn Lane

3

B3055

Setley Plain

PH

SOUTHAMPTON RD

4

459

B3055

LC

A337

Cobblers Corner

SOUTHAMPTON ROAD

Sand

5

Jordans Lane

Widden Bottom

6

Durns Town

B3055 DURNSTOWN

Back Lane

Pitmore Lane

shirley Holms

Jealous

Battrams

7

Birchy

BIRCHY HILL B3055

Lane

Chapel Lane

Coombe

shirley

Shirley holms

shirley R

8

South Sway Lane

Vicarage Lane

Lane

Coombe Lane

Pauls

Kings Lane

King's Farm

Mount Pleasant

Mount Pleasant Lane

Hotel

Mount Pleasant

Mount

Mon Lane

Pleasant

A **B** 488 **C** **D** **E**

I grid square represents 500 metres

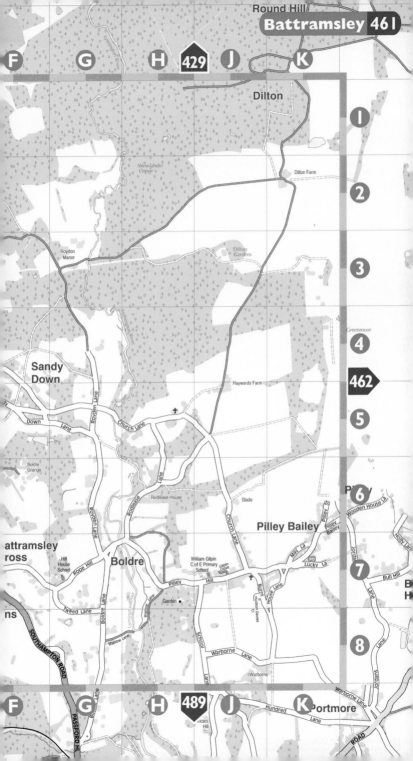

A B 430 C D E

ton

1

Dilton Farm

2

3

Hatchet
Moor

Greenmoor

Beaulieu Heath

4

461

5

B3054

Crockford Bridge

Crockford Stream

Pilley

6

Wooden House La

Norley
Inclosure

ley Bailey

Pilley St

Pilley
Bailey

Mast La

PO
Lu

7

Jordans

Holly Lane

Bull Hill

Bull
Hill

B3054

Norleywood Road

House Lane

8

Jordans
Lane

No
thatcher

Joys La

undred
Lane

Warborne Lane

Portmore

A B 490 C D E

Brook

Hill

Brook

OAD

464

464

LANE B3054

HIGH

CP School

The Lodge

Beaulieu River

Oxleys Copse

The Hummicks

Ot

A

B

432

C

Dock Lane

D

Spearbed Copse

E

I

Beufre Farm

Solent Way

Keeping Copse

Beaulieu River

2

Lane

Lane

3

Ashen Wood

Keeping

Bucklers Hard

PH

4

Lodge Farm

Little Purnel

Tyler's Copse

Clobb

463

5

6

Newlands

Drokes

7

Coopers Wood

St Leonards Grange

8

St Leonards

Solent Way

Bergerie

The Log House

Warren La

A

B

492

C

Park Lane

D

E

Sowley Lane

Thorns Lane

I grid square represents 500 metres

F G H **433** J K

I Langle
Charnwoo

2
We

3

4
466

Exbury
Exbury House

5
Flaxland Pits

6 Inchmery House
Lower Exbury

Gins

7
Beaulieu River

8
Needs Ore Point

F G H **493** J K The Solent
Warren Lane
Warren Farm

Summer Lane
Main Drive
Summer Lane
Gilbury Hard
Yarl Wood
Steepleys Copse
Row Down
Kings Copse Inclosure
Blackwell Common

466

434

465

Blackfield

Tom's Down

Langley

West Common

Lepe

B1
1 Bowland Wy
2 St Francis Cl

C1
1 Foxglade
2 Foxlands
3 Fox's Wk
4 Foxy Paddock
5 Langley Ldg Gdns
6 The Mews

King's Copse Road

Blackwell Common

Whitefield Farm

East Hill Farm

Lepe Farm

Inchmery House

Haxland Pits

Leeds Ore Point

The A...t

I grid square represents 500 metres

A B C D E

1
2
3
4
5
6
7
8

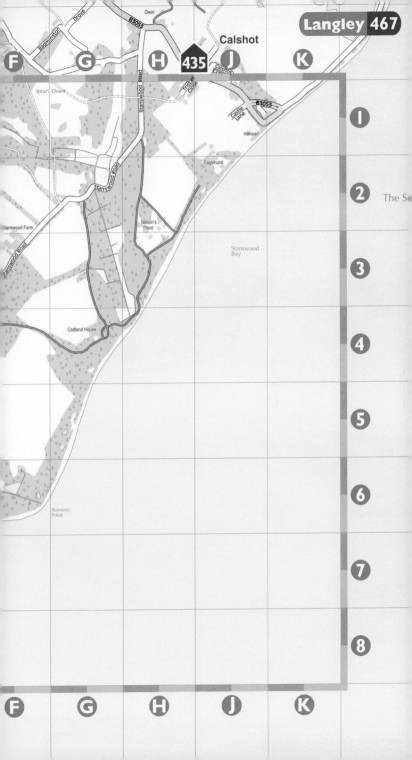

Calshot

435

Ower

B3053

Sprat's Down

Doomkusers

Castle Lane

Hillhead

B3053

Eaglehurst

Stanswood Road

Nelson's Place

Stanswood Bay

Stanswood Farm

Stanswood Road

Cadland House

The S

Stansore Point

F   G   H   J   K

I

2

3

4

5

6

7

8

F   G   H   J   K

468

439

P013

Rown

A2
1 Olave Cl
2 Osborne Rd
3 Queens Cl

A1
1 Inverkip Cl
2 Nottingham Pl
3 Southcliff

B1
1 Chaffinch Wy
2 Common Barn La
3 Empson Wk
4 Kenilworth Cl
cont.

B1 (cont.)
5 Magpie La
6 Martin Cl
7 Sparrow Ct
8 Swallow Ct
9 Swift Cl

B2
1 Chilcomb Cl
2 Esmonde Cl
3 Gibson Cl
4 Harrier Cl
cont.

B2 (cont.)
5 Headley Cl
6 Kimpton Cl
7 Osprey Gdns
8 Trent Wy
9 Waveney Cl

B3
1 Cheyne Wy
2 Maple Cl
3 Trent Wy

C3
1 Larch Cl

C4
1 The Seagulls

E1
1 Connigar Cl

E2
1 Davenport Cl
2 Hudson Cl

Browndown

Browndown
Point

The Sol

1 grid square represents 500 metres

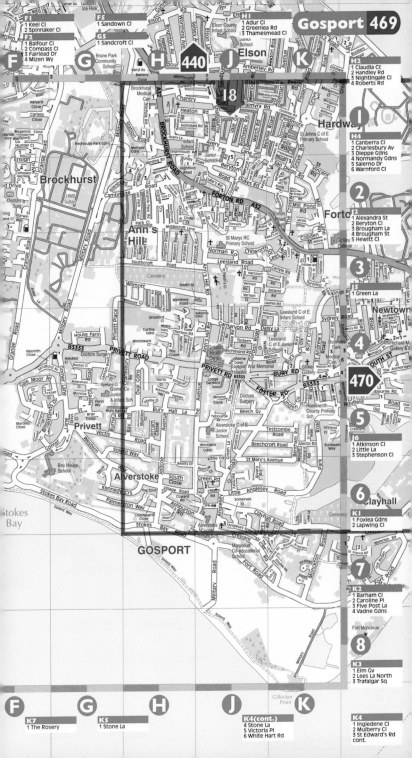

F G H **444** J K

I
2
3
4

Hampshire County

Langstone Channel

Sinah Lake

University of Portsmouth

Ferry Road

Sinah Common

East Winner

Woodlands La

Saltmarsh La

Dover Court

Atheric Road

Charles

Cross

Dennis

West

Copse Cl

Lane

West

Hayfield Drive

Manor

1

4

Culvert

Rd

2

B2025

MANOR

BEACH ROAD

North Shore Road

Hayling Billy Business Cen

Station Theatre

Harbour Road

Warren Cl

Warren Close

Park Road

Lane Cl

Ferry Road

Ferry Road

Sinah La

Links Lane

Catherine

St

St Aubin's Park

Road

St Thomas

St Thomas Av

Avenue

Richmond

PO

Station

474

West Town

Richmond

St Helen's Road

Sea Front

Bacon

Green Lane

Fernhurst

Close

Mayflowers

Westme

5

Balfour

Sea Front

6 **Westfiel**

SOUTH HAYL

7

8

F G H J K

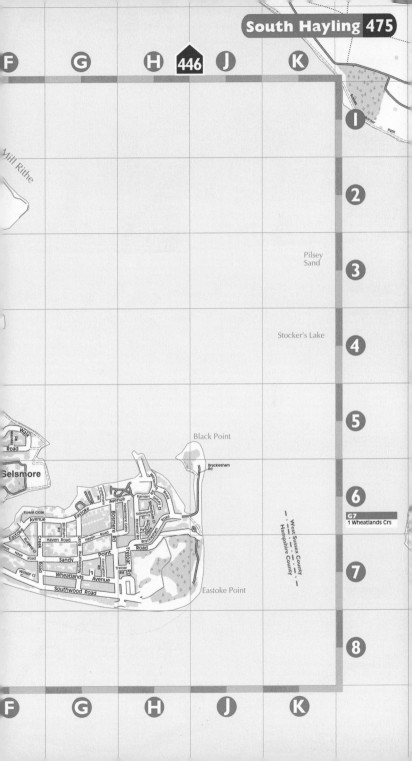

1

2

Pilsey
Sand

3

Stocker's Lake

4

Black Point

5

Brackiesham
Rd

6

G7
1 Wheatlands Crs

West Sussex County
Hampshire County

Mill Rithe

Selsmore

Walk
Seaview
Rd
Road

Rowin Close

Avenue

Eastoke

Avenue

Creek

Haven Road

Eastoke

Eastern Rd

Elm Grove

Flamingo Rd

Bosmere Rd

Haven Road

Nethercote Rd

Earnley

Maisemore Gdns

Paskin Cl

Sidlesham Cl

Treloar
Rd

Brackiesham Road

Bracklesham Rd

Yarfaingo Rd

Richmor Rd

West Have
Road

Windsor Cl

Sandy

Point

Wheatlands

Southwood Road

Avenue

Black Point

Eastoke Point

7

8

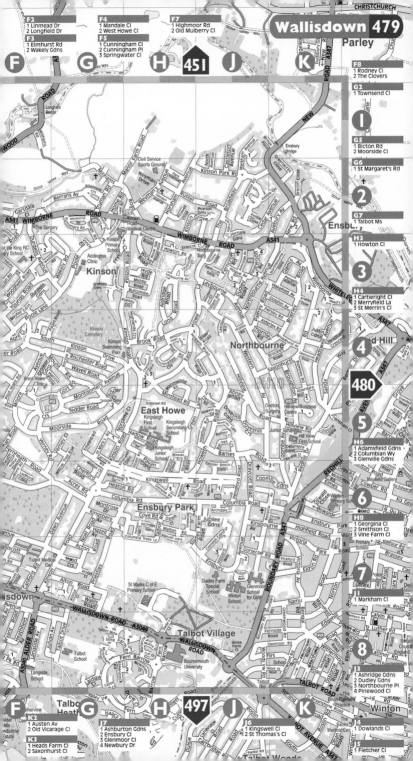

CHRISTCHURCH

West Parley

Parley Cross

B4
1 Castle La West
2 Portswood Dr
3 Redhill Ct
4 The Circle

A8
1 Junction Rd

B3073

PARLEY LA

A7
1 Kilmarnock Rd
2 Lampton Gdns
3 Morden Rd
4 Smithfield Pl
5 St John's Gdns

A4
1 Georgian Wy

A5
1 Old St John's Ms

A B 452 C D E

B5
1 Franklin Rd
2 Malvern Cl
3 Redbreast Rd N
4 Webster Rd

PARLEY LANE

Parley Green

River Stour

I

B6
1 Derwent Cl
2 Forest View Cl
3 Mcwilliam Rd
4 Minterne Rd
5 Rosebud Av

2

B7
1 Garth Rd

Ensbury

Musliff Gdns

Musliff Lane

Muscliff C Primary School

Musliff

3

C4
1 Bosworth Ms
2 Cerne Cl
3 Iwerne Cl
4 Sturminster Rd

WHITELEGG WAY

A347

Wimborne Rd

Newmorton Rd

Granby Road

Boleyn Crescent

Strathmore Rd

Endfield Road

4

Red Hill

WIMBORNE RD

CASTLE LANE WEST A3060

479

AVENUE

A347

RED HILL

Cheddington Road

Shillingstone

Bradford

5

C5
1 Charnwood Av
2 Chickerell Cl
3 Knowlton Gdns
4 Shillingstone Dr

Priory View Road

Castle La West

Broadway

6

C6
1 Charminster Cl
2 Luckham Cl
3 Luckham Pl
4 Luckham Rd East
5 Oakwood Cl

Moordown Medical Cen

Forest View

Haverstock Road

Huntvale

CASTLE LANE WEST A3060

Castle Gate Close

Bournemouth School for Girls

Curlew Road

7

C7
1 Camden Cl
2 West Way Cl

Charminster

CHARMINSTER ROAD

B3063 CHARMINSTER ROAD

Bournemouth School for Boys

Castle Gate Close

Mallard Close

8

C8
1 Cecil Hi

Moordown

Coronation Av

Vicarage Road

Court Road

Sutton Road

Summerbee First School

North Cemetery

Summerbee Second School

D4
1 Gillingham Cl

Pine Road

Gresham Road

Strouden Avenue

Brackendale

D5
1 Durweston Cl

Bishop Road

Rutland Road

Green Road

St Albans Medical Centre

Queen's Park Avenue

West Drive

D6
1 Charminster Pl

Cardigan Road

Parker Road

Fitzharris Avenue

St Alban's Av

St Alba

Queen's Park

E4
1 Barrowgate Rd

A3049

Linwood School

E5
1 Blackfield Rd
2 Bramshaw Gdns
3 Calmore Cl
4 Hungerford Rd

E6
1 Copythorne Cl
2 Landford Gdns
3 Michelmersh Gn
cont.

King's Park

Queen's Pk

I grid square represents 500 metres

F

G

H

453

J

K

Bournemouth International Airport

Dorset County Police

PARLEY LANE
B3073

Merritown

Dales Lane

West Hurn

Hurn Court Lane

Hurn Court Lane

Shoot Lane

Big Lane

Mill Lane

Matchams Lane

Moor Lane

Hurn

PO

Hurn Bridge

B3073

CHRISTCHURCH ROAD

B3073

Avon Causeway

Sopley Common

A338

Blackwater

B3073

A338

Hurn Court

New Bridge

Throop Road

Stour Valley Way

Holdenhurst Road

Holdenhurst

Road

Road

Yeomans Wy

Yeomans Way

Valley Rd

Woodbury

Woodlea House

Surgery

A3060

CASTLE LANE WEST

Craigmoor Avenue

Yeomans Wy

Yeomans Industrial Park

Avenue

Hastings Road

Jewell Road

Throop Road

Stone Wy

Ferrell Gdns

Birch Av

Swanbury Dr

Hopkins Cl

Joyce Lane

Vickers Cl

Hightrees

Leydene Cl

Cooper Dean Dr

Jewell Road

WESSEX WAY

A338

Royal Bournemouth Hospital A&E

Dessington Rd

Bournemouth Crown & County Courts

Littledown Leisure Centre

WESSEX WAY

CASTLE LANE EAST

A3060

Chestnut Av

Walkford

St Peter's School

Trentham Close

F

G

H

499

J

K

Littledown

Portchester School

Avonbourne Girls School

CHRISTCHURCH ROAD

Exton Rd

I
F6
1 Brendon Cl
2 Craigmoor Wy

2
G6
1 Cowdrey Gdns
2 Crantock Gv
3 Culford Cl
4 Mountbatten Rd

3
G8
1 Countess Gdns
2 Sovereign Cl

4
482

5
H7
1 Longbarrow Cl

6
H8
1 The Beeches
2 Eastcott Cl
3 Hazelton Cl

7
I8
1 Bourton Gdns
2 Chandlers Cl
3 Eltham Cl
4 Perryfield Gdns
5 Sparkford Cl

8
K8
1 Hursley Cl

482

A **B** 454 **C** **D** **E**

Court Farm

Avon Causeway

I

A4
1 Valencia Cl
2 Whitby Cl

2

A6
1 Old Barn Cl
2 Squirreis Cl

3

A8
1 Sycamore Cl

Dudmoor Farm

4

481

5

St Catherine's Hill

B8
1 Bernards Cl
2 Eleanor Gdns
3 The Hurdles

Winkton Common

St Catherines's Way

6

C6
1 Lincoln Av

Marsh Lane

Fairmile

7

Bournemouth
Crown & County
Court

C8
1 Adelaide Cl
2 Endfield Rd
3 Kimberley Cl
4 Regency Crs

FAIRMILE ROAD

Christchurch
Hospital

Haworth Cl

8

Jumpers Common

Cemetery

BARRACK ROAD

A **B** 500 **C** **D** **E**

Iford

River Stour

Stour Valley Way

D7
1 Emily Cl
2 Queensmead

D8
1 Latch Farm Av

F

G

H **455**

J

K

BRANSGOR

F5
1 Avon View Rd
2 Harrison Cl
3 Heathlands Cl
4 Kath Chance Cl
5 Kirkham Av
6 Pittmore Rd

Derritt Lane

Wiltshire Gdns
West

Coldust
Close

Westbury Cl

Meyrick Close

Hill Cl

Burley Road

Harrow Road

Brook La

1

F6
1 Barlands Cl
2 Summerfield Cl

North Bockhampton

Neacroft

Hampshire County
Dorset County

Lr Clockhouse Farm

2

BH23

F7
1 Burton Cl

Bockhampton Road

Middle Bockhampton

Burley Road

3

Winkton

Burley Road

South Bockhampton

Lyndhurst Road

Wate

G5
1 Burton Hall Pl

Homefield School

Waterditch Road

4

484

Waterditch Farm

Waterditch Road

5

Salisbury Road

Primary School

The Lindens

Preston Lane

G6
1 Woodstock Rd

Moorcro
Av

Vinneys

Burton Medical Cen

Vicarage Way

Hawthorn Road

Hill Lane

Dorset County

Hampshire County

6

Priory

Crabtree

Footners Lane

Whitenayes Cl

Godowen Rd

Treedys

Whitenayes Road

Burton

Holly Gdns

Summers Lane

G7
1 Martins Hill La

Hill Alder Lane

Medlar

Salisbury Road

Valley Lane

7

LYNDHURST

G8
1 Sarah Sands Cl

B3347

Sandy Plot

Stapleclose

Ambury

Dorset Road

Hunt

CHRISTCHURCH BY-PASS A35

Valley Lane

Westcliffe
Gdns

8

HIGHCLIFFE ROAD A337

Saffron

CHRISTCHURCH

V-vine Lane

Everest Road

St Josephs RC School

Edward Road

Edward Rd

Kingsley House Surg.

B3059

Somerford Rd

Sea Vixen Industrial Est

Grange Road Business Cen

Christchurch Business Cen

F

Purew G

Grange Comprehensive School

Christchurch Medical Centre

H **501**

I

Junior Sch

Infant School

J

Somerford
ROAD

Somer
Business Park

K

Hunter
Cl

Brazabon Dr

Silver Business Park

K1
1 Meadow Cl

REWELL

J8
1 Charles Rd
2 Coleridge Gn

H8
1 Bonington Cl
2 Hillary Rd

SOMERFORD

Airfield

Way

Beaver

Moffat Rd

Christchurch Business Cen

484

456

BR A GORE B C D E

Twin Oaks Medical Cen

Westbury Cl

A7
1 Columbine Cl
2 Monkshood Cl

I

St Mary's Close

Bransgore Primary School

Beech House

Harrow Road

Harrow Lodge

Neacroft

Lyndhurst Road

2

A8
1 Bellflower Cl
2 Honeysuckle Wy
3 Speedwell Dr

Chisels Croft La

Ringwood Road

Godswinscroft

Lyndhurst Road

3

B8
1 Clematis Cl
2 Foxglove Cl

Waterditch

4

Waterditch Road

Waterditch F

483

Hill Lane

Burton Common

5

C7
1 Fir Tree La
2 Winsford Cl

A35

LYNDHU

Station Road

6

Hampshire

Dorset Cl

C8
1 Burnside
2 Farmdene Cl
3 Harriers Cl
4 Saulfland Pl

A35

Hintonwood

Hinton Admiral Station

The Meadway

Havelock Wy

LYNDHURST ROAD

7

D7
1 Birchwood Cl
2 Milverton Cl

Sundew Close

Westfield Gdns

St Josephs RC School

ward RD

Kingsley House Surg.

8

Sea Vixen Industrial Est

B3059

Somerford Business Park

Hughes Business Cen

Grange Road Business Cen

Christchurch Business Cen

HIGHCLIFFE ROAD A337

Saffron

Hoburne Lane

Smugglers

A GORE B 502 C D E

LYMINGTON RD

N RD Y HL

Wellin

Highcliffe Castle

LYMIN

D8
1 Knightwood Cl

E8
1 Angeline Cl
2 Norleywood

1 grid square represents 500 metres

F Farm   **G**   **H**   **457**   **J**   **K**

North Drive

South Drive

Holm Hill Lane

1
F6
1 Beckley Copse

2
G6
1 Clinton Cl
2 Nicholas Cl
3 Wyndham Cl

Ossemsley Manor

3
G7
1 Gordon Mt
2 Walkford Wy

Birch Av

Lawn View

BASHLEY

Vintage Motorcycle Museum

Bashley Manor Farm

BASHLEY CROSS

Beckley

Beckley Farm

B3055

Hinton

Hinton Lane

Hinton House

Velvet Lawn

Doe Copse

Stem Lane

4
Hazelwood
Avenue
Kennard

Beech W

New Milton

486
Marsh
Maryat

Walkford Brook

Walkford Lane

Stem Lane

Brier Cl

Charles worth

Arundel

Queensway

5
G8
1 Jay's Ct

Brownsea

Wick 1 Industrial Est

Wick 2 Industrial Est

Nova Business Pk

Fawcett

Charnock Close

LC

6
New Milton
J8
1 Rockbourne Gdn
2 Sellwood Wy
3 Studley Ct

Gore Road

Cemetery

Arnewood School

Old Milton

Old Milton

OLD MILTON GN

Southviews Walk

7
K3
3 1 Cherry Tree Dr

Plantation

Glenville

Southwood

Walkford

Chewton Farm Road

Avenue Road

Walkford Road

Arran Way

Highland Av

Birchdale Cl

Jacobean Close

Highcliffe

Chewton Common

Station Road

Police Station

Stuart Road

Montagu Road

Bure Drive

Abington Drive

Studley Close

Lodge

The Dell

Bartonside Rd

The Crescent

Field Place

Glen

Westcroft

CHRISTCHURCH ROAD

A337

Christchurch Road

Barton Court Road

Knight Park

Chiltern

Parkland Drive

Three Acre Dr

Elton

Wavendon Drive

8
Hengistbury Road

Seacroft Av

Pine

Seafield Road

Carlton Av

Fairfield Road

Keysworth

Barton Close

Angois Close

Seafield Close

Barton Dr

Beach Avenue

Marine

Hotel

Marine Drive West

K8
1 Christchurch Rd
2 Dunford Cl

K5
1 Breamore Cl
2 Hatfield Ct
3 Stratfield Pl
4 Thoresby Ct

K4
M 1 The Hyde

486

458

A7
1 Manor Farm Cl
2 Moore Cl
3 Prestwood Cl
4 Wendover Cl

A6
1 Goldfinch Cl
2 Magpie Gv
3 Wagtail Dr
4 Wren Cl

A5
1 Balmoral Wk
2 Brooklyn Ct
3 Foxcote Gdns
4 Linnet Ct
5 Wilton Gdns

A4
1 Deer Park Cl
2 Rosecrae Cl

1

B4
1 Forest Pines

B6
1 Derrybrian Gdns

2

B7
1 Spindlewood Cl

C2
1 Kamptee Copse

3

C3
1 Marston Cl

C6
1 Arden Wk
2 Rothbury Pk
3 Stannington Cl

4

New Mi **485**

5

C7
1 Baden Cl
2 Greenwoods

C8
1 Arlington Ct
2 Hedgerley
3 Seaway

6

D4
1 Acorn Cl
2 Burnleigh Gdns
3 Hawthorn Cl
4 Pilgrim Cl
5 Prince's Pl

Old Milton

7

D5
1 Daneswood Rd
2 Homewood Cl
3 Melrose Ct

8

D6
1 Ashdown Wk

E4
1 Bailey Cl
2 Denmead
3 Dinham Rd
4 Foxglove Pl
5 Sundew Cl

504

E5
1 Somerton Cl

E6
1 Springfield Gdns

1 grid square represents 500 metres

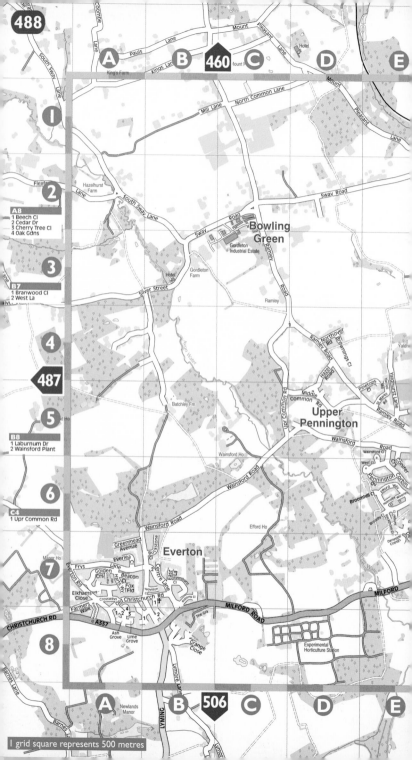

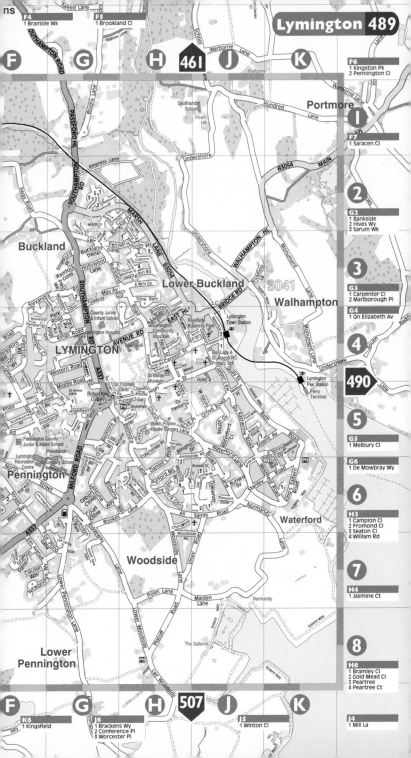

Needs
Ore Point

The Solent

Warren Lane

Warren Farm

s House

465

F G H J K

1
2
3
4
5
6
7
8

F G H J K

494

476

1 grid square represents 500 metres

496

478

495

509

Newtown

Rossmore

Branksom

Ashley

Parkstone

Brank
Park

Lilliput

Canford Cliffs

1 grid square represents 500 metres

Talbot Village

479

F2
1 Guest Cl

F3
1 Yarmouth Cl

F6
1 Leicester Rd

Winton

I

G5
1 Eldon Pl
2 Seamoor La

2

G6
1 Drury Rd
2 Grovely Rd

3

H1
1 Bishop Cl

4

498

5

H5
1 Heatherbank Rd
2 Landseer Rd

6

H7
1 Crosby Rd

7

J4
1 Kensington Dr

8

J5
1 Suffolk Rd South

Poole Bay

K6
1 Durley Rd South
2 Durley Rbt
3 Hahnemann Rd
4 Kerley Rd
5 South View Pl
6 West Cliff Gdns

K5
1 Mannington Pl
2 Orchard St
3 The Triangle
4 West Hill Pl

K4
1 Durrant Rd

498

A **B** **480** **C** **D** **E**

Winton

1

BH3 **22** **23**

2

3

BH

4

Springbourne

BH1

497

WESSEX

CHRISTCHURCH

5

6

BOURNEMOUTH

Poole
Bay

7

8

A **B** **C** **D** **E**

I grid square represents 500 metres

F

G

H

481

J

K

I

2

3

West

1 Henley Gdns

4

500

5

6

7

8

F

G

H

J

K

502

HIGHCLIFF **A**   **B**   **484**   **C**   **D**   **E**

484

LYMINGTON RD
SHELLEY HL
A337

Friars
Cliff

Homage

Mudeford

Highcliffe
Medical
Centre

Capesthorne

1

2

3

4

501

5

6

7

8

A   **B**   **C**   **D**   **E**

Barton on Sea

I grid square represents 500 metres

495

A · B · C · D · E

I

Poole
Harbour

Poole
Dorset County

2

3

Maryland

The
Villa

Middle   Street

Brownsea
Island (NT)

BH13

4

+

5

Furzey
Island

BH15

6

Green
Island

BH15

Brand's
Bay

7

South
Deep

Jerry's
Point

8

Goathorn
Plantation

Ferry Road

A · B · C · D · E

I grid square represents 500 metres

USING THE STREET INDEX

Street names are listed alphabetically. Each street name is followed by its postal town or area locality, the Postcode District, the page number, and the reference to the square in which the name is found.

Example: **Abbey Cl** *FAWY* SO45 ....**169** H5 ▣

Some entries are followed by a number in a blue box. This number indicates the location of the street within the referenced grid square. The full street name is listed at the side of the map page.

ENERAL ABBREVIATIONS

...ACCESS	GA	GATE	PL	PLACE
...ALLEY	GAL	GALLERY	PLN	PLAIN
...APPROACH	GDN	GARDEN	PLNS	PLAINS
...ARCADE	GDNS	GARDENS	PLZ	PLAZA
...ASSOCIATION	GLD	GLADE	POL	POLICE STATION
...AVENUE	GLN	GLEN	PR	PRINCE
...BEACH	GN	GREEN	PREC	PRECINCT
S...BUILDINGS	GND	GROUND	PREP	PREPARATORY
...BEND	GRA	GRANGE	PRIM	PRIMARY
...BANK	GRG	GARAGE	PROM	PROMENADE
...BRIDGE	GT	GREAT	PRS	PRINCESS
...BROOK	GTWY	GATEWAY	PRT	PORT
...BOTTOM	GV	GROVE	PT	POINT
...BUSINESS	HGR	HIGHER	PTH	PATH
...BOULEVARD	HL	HILL	PZ	PIAZZA
...BYPASS	HLS	HILLS	QD	QUADRANT
H...CATHEDRAL	HO	HOUSE	QU	QUEEN
...CEMETERY	HOL	HOLLOW	QY	QUAY
...CENTRE	HOSP	HOSPITAL	R	RIVER
...CROFT	HRB	HARBOUR	RBT	ROUNDABOUT
...CHURCH	HTH	HEATH	RD	ROAD
...CHASE	HTS	HEIGHTS	RDG	RIDGE
'D...CHURCHYARD	HVN	HAVEN	REP	REPUBLIC
...CIRCLE	HWY	HIGHWAY	RES	RESERVOIR
...CIRCUS	IMP	IMPERIAL	RFC	RUGBY FOOTBALL CLUB
...CLOSE	IN	INLET	RI	RISE
...CLIFFS	IND EST	INDUSTRIAL ESTATE	RP	RAMP
...CAMP	INF	INFIRMARY	RW	ROW
...CORNER	INFO	INFORMATION	S	SOUTH
...COUNTY	INT	INTERCHANGE	SCH	SCHOOL
...COLLEGE	IS	ISLAND	SE	SOUTH EAST
...COMMON	JCT	JUNCTION	SER	SERVICE AREA
M...COMMISSION	JTY	JETTY	SH	SHORE
...CONVENT	KG	KING	SHOP	SHOPPING
...COTTAGE	KNL	KNOLL	SKWY	SKYWAY
S...COTTAGES	L	LAKE	SMT	SUMMIT
...CAPE	LA	LANE	SOC	SOCIETY
...COPSE	LDG	LODGE	SP	SPUR
...CREEK	LGT	LIGHT	SPR	SPRING
M...CREMATORIUM	LK	LOCK	SQ	SQUARE
...CRESCENT	LKS	LAKES	ST	STREET
Y...CAUSEWAY	LNDG	LANDING	STN	STATION
...COURT	LTL	LITTLE	STR	STREAM
...CENTRAL	LWR	LOWER	STRD	STRAND
...COURTS	MAG	MAGISTRATE	SW	SOUTH WEST
...COURTYARD	MAN	MANSIONS	TDG	TRADING
...CUTTINGS	MD	MEAD	TER	TERRACE
...COVE	MDW	MEADOWS	THWY	THROUGHWAY
...CANYON	MEM	MEMORIAL	TNL	TUNNEL
T...DEPARTMENT	MKT	MARKET	TOLL	TOLLWAY
...DALE	MKTS	MARKETS	TPK	TURNPIKE
...DAM	ML	MALL	TR	TRACK
...DRIVE	ML	MILL	TRL	TRAIL
...DROVE	MNR	MANOR	TWR	TOWER
...DRIVEWAY	MS	MEWS	U/P	UNDERPASS
GS...DWELLINGS	MSN	MISSION	UNI	UNIVERSITY
...EAST	MT	MOUNT	UPR	UPPER
...EMBANKMENT	MTN	MOUNTAIN	V	VALE
BY...EMBASSY	MTS	MOUNTAINS	VA	VALLEY
...ESPLANADE	MUS	MUSEUM	VIAD	VIADUCT
...ESTATE	MWY	MOTORWAY	VIL	VILLA
...EXCHANGE	N	NORTH	VIS	VISTA
Y...EXPRESSWAY	NE	NORTH EAST	VLG	VILLAGE
...EXTENSION	NW	NORTH WEST	VLS	VILLAS
...FLYOVER	O/P	OVERPASS	VW	VIEW
...FOOTBALL CLUB	OFF	OFFICE	W	WEST
...FORK	ORCH	ORCHARD	WD	WOOD
...FIELD	OV	OVAL	WHF	WHARF
S...FIELDS	PAL	PALACE	WK	WALK
...FALLS	PAS	PASSAGE	WKS	WALKS
...FLATS	PAV	PAVILION	WLS	WELLS
...FARM	PDE	PARADE	WY	WAY
...FORT	PH	PUBLIC HOUSE	YD	YARD
...FREEWAY	PK	PARK	YHA	YOUTH HOSTEL
...FERRY	PKWY	PARKWAY		

OSTCODE TOWNS AND AREA ABBREVIATIONS

T...Aldershot	BROC	Brockenhurst	CWTH	Crowthorne
N...Alton	BSTK	Basingstoke	DEAN	Deane/Oakley
SY...Amesbury	BWD	Bearwood	ELGH	Eastleigh
...Andover	CBLY	Camberley	EMRTH	Emsworth/Southbourne
V...Ash Vale	CCLF	Canford Cliffs	ENEY	Eastney
T...Broadstone	CFDH	Canford Heath	EPSF	Petersfield east
E/WDN...Branksome/Wallisdown	CHAM	Cosham	EWKG	Wokingham east
W...Blackwater	CHAR	Charminster	FARN	Farnborough
TH...Bournemouth	CHCH/BSGR	Christchurch/Bransgore	FAWY	Fawley/Hythe
...Bordon	CHFD	Chandler's Ford	FBDG	Fordingbridge
C...Boscombe	CHIN	Chineham	FERN	Ferndown/West Moors
VT...Bishop's Waltham	CHOB/PIR	Chobham/Pirbright	FHAM	Fareham

10th - Air

Index - streets

A